A Galloway Childhood

Books by
Ian Niall

No Resting Place
Foxhollow
Tune on a Melodeon
The Poacher's Handbook
The Deluge
Fresh Woods
Pastures New
The Boy Who Saw Tomorrow
A Tiger Walks
The New Poacher's Handbook
Trout From the Hills
The Harmless Albatross
Hey, Delaney!
The Gamekeeper
Country Blacksmith
A Galloway Childhood
The Galloway Shepherd

as
John McNeillie

Wigtown Ploughman
Glasgow Keelie
Morryham Farm

A Galloway Childhood

by

Ian Niall

First published 1967
This edition 2000

Copyright Ian Niall

ISBN 1 872350 13 5

Published by
G.C.Book Publishers Ltd
17 North Main Street,
Wigtown,
Scotland DG8 9HL

Printed and bound in Great Britain by
MPG Books Ltd, Bodmin, Cornwall

Grandfather

1

Tall Trees and Bright Mornings

It would be hard for me to prove that the mornings of my childhood were brighter than mornings now, or that the trees were taller, and the little round hills greener than they are today. If sepia portraits tend to fade that is because a chemical change is taking place and perhaps because the light at the time the photograph was taken was lacking in strength, but the Galloway of which I write here was a magic world, with blue, far-off hills, hills that were grey and hills that were purple, and moorland wilderness above which the eagle slowly flew or sailed in a graceful circle — for the eagle, now newly returned to the south-west, was there when I was a child. My relations (I should say my elders) were bigger men than I see today and the womenfolk more maternal, even if they smelt of camphor balls and creaked in whalebone stays, and wore, as my grandmother did, hats as big and bulky as a carrion-crow's nest.

I wasn't born in Galloway, which comprises Wigtownshire and the Stewartry of Kirkcudbright, nor yet in Kyle, but farther north. My father was born in Galloway and his family had been there as long as there had been parish records, and even longer. It didn't do to whisper that they might have originated anywhere else, a great-aunt or uncle having come across the water from Ireland, and indeed no one did. With the passing of more than half my years I understand the colourful imagination they had, the gift for turning a phrase and if it wasn't exactly Irish it was certain Gaelic in descriptiveness.

'The morn's morn,' my grandfather would say to one of his men, 'you'll take old Bob and go up to the moss and cut a wheen of peats against the winter's cold.' And in the morning the man would go to the peat moss and cut some peats to be aired and dried and finally brought home to give us a winter fire so hot, so aromatic and so oxygen consuming, that the entire family would fall asleep in their chairs after supper and only awake when the wick of the oil lamp had burned low and the grey ash of the peats had finally fallen through the bars of the grate.

I came very small and very young into this world. I never seriously questioned my mother why this happened. It was a delicate point with her. She had been persuaded that the country air and country food would be good for me. It seems that I was a somewhat sickly child and couldn't keep my food down. I had need of something better than the smoky atmosphere of towns and I left them before I was eighteen months old. Although my mother spent many years worrying whether I would go through life with a ploughman's slouch and was a little troubled that I knew so much about the breeding of animals, I bless the day she set me down in my grandfather's household where the cats crowded the hearth, the canary bird sang to burst his heart and the comings and goings of the family made the farm kitchen as busy as any place I have ever known since. How enthusiastically we lived, how cold it was on those winter mornings when the pump had to be thawed with a great kettle of boiling water, and how peaceful it was on Sunday, when they went off to the kirk with the pony specially groomed, the harness polished, the brass and gig lamps burnished and Grandmother and Grandfather 'decked off' in their Sunday clothes.

Ours was a God-fearing household. My grandfather never used an oath and he never blasphemed, but he did curse, or, to be more exact, he used one curse that served for all occasions. I am not sure that it wasn't a prayer. When taxed to the extreme he would throw whatever he had in his hand on to the floor or dash it upon the ground, and look heavenward, imploring God to damn whatever it was to hell! I am not sure whether God paid great heed to him, for he was inclined to make this appeal rather often, being a hot-tempered and impatient man, but when I made the same prayer myself in my mother's presence she, good soul, was cast down in grief I was, after all, barely three years old,

North Clutag Steading, with Grandfather harnessing Tammy to the rig.

rather young to be calling upon God for such drastic assistance in overcoming my infant frustrations. Dashing my bonnet on the ground at the same time struck Mother as imitating my grandfather rather than imploring my maker from deep religious conviction. My father, to whom my shortcomings were reported, was saddened by the effect my unusual upbringing was having upon me, but he couldn't deny that I was loved, nay worshipped, by the family. They fed and nourished me, measured me week by week to see how I was growing towards a lamp that was fixed on a bracket on the wall, and brushed and combed my flaxen locks to make me presentable for company when the minister called. They gave me veterinary tomes to amuse me when they were too hard pressed to play with me themselves. I loved the diagrams of the blood circulation of cows that lifted up to reveal the animal's stomach and bowels in blue, purple and green. I loved the hen that came stalking in through the open door to mark the newly washed flags and the collie dog that awoke and discovered the intruder and chased her out again with so much disturbance that the whole floor had to be washed over once more. I loved every day I lived in that place for it inspired in me an appreciation of the simple and unsophisticated things of life. By the time I was taken away to live in my father's house I had been indelibly impressed with something that could only be described as peasant environment. There are fewer peasants these days and for some reason those who are indisputably of peasant origin, as indeed more than ninety per cent of the people of this country must surely be, find something amusing or shameful in the admission that they come of peasant stock. I am not sure that I can rightfully call myself a peasant but I am very proud of my origins among peasants, for they were a virile, vigorous, hard-to-kill, resourceful people. Blood is thicker than water, they say. It is a poor phrase to give an indication of the closeness of the family in which I spent my formative years. I trust the reader will understand this, and much more, by the time he has travelled back with me to the existence I knew in Galloway as a small child.

2

Run, You Wee Beggars!

My mother's father was an adventuresome man. He had crossed the Atlantic as a boy, signing on as a member of the crew of a sailing-ship when he was no more than thirteen years of age. He sailed barefooted for he hadn't the money for seaboots. Since crossings were generally made in summer this may not have been as drastic as it sounds. Mother displayed a little of her father's undauntability by going down to Galloway to meet my father's family for the first time quite alone. For some reason my father was persuaded that they would all get on a great deal better if his wife-to-be met them without his being there at her side. He stayed behind in Glasgow and Mother set off for grey Galloway on a bleak winter's day.

She had caught but a brief glimpse of it once before when she had sailed to the west coast of Ireland with her father and she expected a grey, mist-shrouded country with brooding crags and wild, lonely stretches of moorland that finally, almost on the edge of the sea, would give place to a dairy-farming countryside fast in the grip of winter. The railway was no more infallible then than it is now. The train ran late, huffed and puffed its way through the vales and fir-plantings of Ayrshire and at last came to a steaming halt on a gradient flanked by a rocky cutting. It would climb no more; it was hot and tired and its big iron tyres slipped on the icy rails though they whirled madly and did their best to take hold. Slowly the train slid back. Passengers in compartments to the rear wiped the condensation from the windows and wondered what it was all about. Passengers situated nearer the head of the train opened windows and peered up the track, breathing the lung-searing cold air and consulting their watches, for it was plain that those who were going all the way were going to be very late indeed. The driver and the fireman were unable to raise more steam. What the train needed was an extra engine.

Mother ate the last of her sandwiches and watched the shadows gathering in the trees above the cutting. She would see a black Galloway before she saw it in the light of day. A feeling of depression settled upon her. She felt far less confident than her father had been when he sailed out of the Clyde, a barefoot boy before the mast. There was another problem. She wondered if anyone would wait until the train came. It could be hours, a fellow-passenger told her. Another engine would have to get steam up and be brought to the scene, and it didn't follow that even two locomotives would solve the problem! The condensation was freezing on the windows for the heat was diminishing. What could they expect when the driver was squandering the steam in great clouds?

By the time a second engine arrived the compartment was quite cold and passengers all along the train had grown weary of hauling up the windows and looking out into the night. The second engine startled the dispirited travellers when it steamed up and made contact with the rear of the stationary train, and then, after a brief interval for consultation between guard and drivers, the train moved on again. The wheels rang with a metallic complaint as the two engines fought to overcome the gradient, and at last the incline was passed. The engines allowed more steam to escape than they had done while climbing the slope, the pushing locomotive was uncoupled and the journey resumed. Long hours had passed. My mother's little fob-watch, which she had inspected continuously at first, but had given up looking at for some time, suggested the train's arrival would be delayed still more by the disruption of local services and the connection Mother had to make on the Wigtownshire Railway. She might just as well have been on her way to Siberia, it seemed. When she wiped the window to look out into the night she could see little but the stars and black outlines of crags and firwoods, and here and there, far out in the depths of the night, a light from a cottage or farmhouse window sailing back like a slowly moving comet or shooting star.

It wasn't only the traveller to Galloway who was put out by the failure of the train to climb a frozen track. My grandfather had set out in the late afternoon to meet the connection that should have brought my mother. He was accompanied by one of my aunts-to-be and both were dressed for the occasion. Grandfather's large boots had been polished until they shone like mirrors. His beard had been trimmed and groomed. He wore his best tweed suit (woven from the wool of his own sheep) and a cravat that masked half of a stiff white dicky. His heavy topcoat was turned up to shelter his ears but he wasn't wearing his hard hat. That would have been too formal. Hard hats were for funerals and sombre occasions. He wore his best heavy tweed cap and smoked a silver-lidded pipe. The pony, too, had been groomed and prepared with as much care as my aunt-to-be had given to her bonnet and other feminine adornments. The gig shone and the lamps were burnished. The brass glittered in the reflections of the shining harness. Father and daughter were wrapped in travelling-rugs. The gig was steered clear of potholes on the rough farm road and driven with Grandfather's usual pride in his horsemanship once it trundled on to the public road. They had five or six miles to go. They expected the train to be a little late but they weren't exactly prepared for such a long delay.

Greylags were coming off the meadows along the Bladnoch's side, flying in long trailing skeins and with a great musical babbling that geese make when they take to the air. They circled and climbed, swimming upward into the western sky that was just beginning to be shaded by the sunset. When they had gone it was strangely hushed and silent along the freezing road. The land was bare; the last pheasant had picked his way across the field and gone to roost in the trees, the last hare hopped into the shelter of the hedge or the reeds. Grandfather stopped humming to himself and fumbled in the layers of his clothing to bring out his watch. Just how late the train was began to be indicated by the silence. He knew when to expect the far-away hushing sound

13

of its progress through hills and alongside woods. He had often timed it, as it journeyed from one landmark to another, and all by sound, on a crisp, cold day when there was but the slightest breeze. When they came at last to the bridge, and then to the tail of the village, he let the pony's pace slacken.

On the way up the street he stopped for a dram. It put new warmth in his bones. What it did for my aunt-to-be was also apparent. It put a look of strong disapproval on her face. He was a too-jolly man when he was warmed by a dram. She wanted him to be on his best behaviour for this meeting. What would the young women think if he greeted her reeking of whisky? She herself would be 'fair affronted'! He might have gone without his dram, cold though the twilight was, Grandfather, however, paid no heed to his daughter's forbidding expression. He talked to the pony and now and then, as they went on up the long street, bade good evening to acquaintances and exchanged comments about the duration of the bitterly cold spell.

At the station, a mile or so beyond, they got down and consulted the 'station-master and ticket-collector'. He was busy manhandling churns and blowing on his hands between times. His watch was compared with Grandfather's. A bell began ringing in the little office at the end of the white-painted fence. Bells were ringing all along the railway and remarks were being made about the inefficiency of other lines. It wasn't the first time that a train had got stuck in the wilds of Ayrshire. Grandfather's information was the best he could get. He turned the gig about and went briskly back down to the long street where he gave a boy a sixpence to hold the pony. Here father and daughter parted company. Grandfather went for his second 'wee half' and my aunt-to-be went visiting a friend who plied her with biscuits and tea, neither of which did much to relieve her anxiety concerning the impression Grandfather would make on my father's intended.

The last stage of Mother's train journey seemed longer than all that had gone before because it seemed that she would never arrive. The train fussed and fumed, slowed down and rolled on again, without attaining a reasonable speed. The driver might have been admiring the great bowl of night patterned by a million stars. Mother stared at the button-studded upholstery without the slightest idea of the distance that remained to be covered. When the train finally came to a halt she sat for some minutes without realizing that they were at a station. The world outside was as dark as ever but when she heard someone talking in the unfamiliar Wigtownshire accent she opened the door of the compartment and saw that there was a platform. At the far end of the platform a dim light blinked. She struggled to get her luggage down. She was well used to the northern winter but it seemed at that moment that Galloway was the coldest and most inhospitable place on the earth. No one came to help her with her bag. She stood forlornly peering at the lamp, wondering where the exit from the platform was, but then she discerned the bulk of a man in a topcoat coming towards her.

'Is that you, lassie?' he asked.

It was a question she hesitated to answer but she said, 'Yes, it's me.'

The big bearded man took her bag and she hurried at his side as he plodded up the platform. As an afterthought he spoke her name. She was Jeannie. The fact was established. She sighed with relief. She had begun to have a serious apprehension that she might have made a mistake, misrepresenting herself to a complete stranger who was about to hurry her away to some even darker and unknown part of the countryside. Grandfather bade the ticket-collector have done with his fumbling with mailbags and come and let his future daughter-in-law surrender her ticket according to the rule. Mother went through the gate to meet Father's sister and be helped up into the jumble of travelling-rugs.

'She's late,' said Grandfather. He was talking of the train but Mother felt that she was being personally reproached for not coming on foot and arriving nearer the appointed hour. The pony was turned about, Mother caught the handrail to steady herself and felt her bag rolling heavily on to her feet, for the well of the

15

trap was not very roomy and Grandfather's feet were firmly planted to hold the restive pony so eager to be off at the gallop. They went up the slope to the road and began to turn at the bridge. At that moment the train moved out and gave an angry belch as it passed underneath. The pony stood on his hind legs and his forefeet pawed the air. The gig ran back and everything in it tumbled towards the door but Grandfather had been in this situation before and hauled on the reins, pulling the pony's head down on to his chest.

'To hell!' he shouted above the rumble of the train, 'you'd think they'd have the sense to wait until we were off the bridge!'

Mother had never been so frightened in her life. On one side of the narrow bridge the pony's forelegs had hung above the railway and on the other the rear of the gig had ground against the stone wall; but all was soon well, the gig squared about and progress homeward resumed. Grandfather began to sing and continued to do so despite his daughter's plea that he should be quiet and not show that he had taken a dram. Although Grandfather was hardly ever in his life fuddled or to any degree overcome by drink, when he had taken a dram he was not to be put down.

'Hold your wheesht, lassie,' he said, 'and let me sing!'

And sing he did, so that when they came again to the long street of the village the urchins came out of the doorways and the shadows to run beside the gig and plead for pennies. They knew him well and called to him as they ran. It was a bitterly cold night but they were barefoot and they padded along the hard road hoping that if he tossed them a few pennies they would be able to find them, even in the dark. The street was lit by one lamp and here and there the light from a window. Grandfather laughed and called to the boys whose numbers grew as the pony pricked up its ears and quickened its pace.

'Run, ye wee buggers!' he urged. 'Run!'

Mother smiled in the darkness. Her future sister-inlaw pretended to be as shocked as she might have been had she heard that wicked word for the first time in her life.

'Run, ye wee buggers!

A few pennies jingled and rattled on to the frozen street and then a few more. The boys scrambled and grovelled and fought to get them, rolling over in heaps, and the more persistent runners tried to grab the door of the trap and stay with it until Grandfather could be persuaded to part with more of his change, which he did when they had run out of the long street and were on the dark road to the bridge and the fir-plantings.

'Thank ye, mister,' they called into the night. Grandfather began to sing again, drowning his daughter's scolding words. He had enjoyed being himself and showing Mother that he had no intention of pretending to be anything else. Mother had quite recovered from the discomfort she had experienced on the railway bridge. She was a little apprehensive when the pony's feet slipped on the icy road and Grandfather told it to take its time and not spill them all out. He had a habit of talking to his horse in a way that intrigued everyone who drove with him. The horse enjoyed a one-sided conversation that left anyone who heard it in no doubt that Grandfather considered horses at least man's equal in intelligence and capable of understanding every word he said. This also made Mother a little uneasy. It had never entered her head that anyone might seriously consider an animal on his own level. The pony evidently understood for it did exactly as it was advised to do, slowed in some places, held the weight in his collar, trundled the gig on to the verge.

'Have you ever smelt air like it?' asked Grandfather. Mother took a breath of unbelievably cold air and said she hadn't, which was probably true. The cottages they were passing were burning peat and there is no scent more wonderful than the smoke of a peat fire mingling with the cold air of a winter's night.

They came to the farm road in due time. The gig rocked a little as they turned off and headed up the slope into the dark fields that led to the marches of Clutag. Obediently my aunt-to-be got down and opened the gates. Mother was reaching her destination hours late. Grandmother would have looked down the road a thousand times in the hope of seeing the candlelit gig lamps indicating their imminent arrival, and heaped more peat on the fire so that the radiance and warmth of her welcome would be complete and undiminished. Mother saw at last the lamp in the window and the sombre outline of the outbuildings, the byre gable, the long white wall of the stable and cartshed. The gig came to a rocking halt and, rather stiffly, Mother stepped down. Grandfather went off to unyoke his pony and run the gig into the gighouse. Mother followed her future sister-in-law into the house, smelling the baking, the mouth-watering savoury smell of roasted chicken. The house shone. Grandmother hurried to greet her and take her coat. They smiled at one another. In the passageway between sitting-room and kitchen one of Father's sisters told the other how Grandfather had let the family down, taking a dram, reeking of whisky, encouraging the ragged boys of the village to run at their heels and scramble for pennies while he urged them on with words that were unfit for the ears of a young woman from the town. Grandmother ignored the mumbling in the passage. This was her son's intended wife, come all the way from Glasgow, a stranger in a strange place and not used to the ways of country folk.

When she had done justice to an enormous spread, sampled the rich cake, shortbread, apple tart and oven scones, and had the opportunity of seeing Grandfather at the head of the table, still with the glow of the dram reddening his cheeks, Mother retired to bed in a downstairs bedroom reserved for special guests and containing some enormous mahogany furniture. It took her a long time to get to sleep. She was unused to the chiming of grandfather clocks that weren't exactly synchronized and not at all used to an owl hissing and rumbling about in the chimney. Before morning she awoke in sheer horror at an unearthly sound coming from the window. She lay until daylight, petrified. It turned out that it was the habit of a particular horse to force his way out of the little paddock and lick the windowpanes on the ground floor. Mother smiled weakly at the explanation and wished Father had accompanied her on the visit.

She wished this even more in the days that followed when she was taken on a tour of her future relations and sat down to more

Nightfall at North Clutag

feasts of scone, fruit cake, shortbread and other sorts of confectionery in which farmers' wives took pride. Her appetite was remarked upon when she departed. Townsfolk all had puny appetites and a nervousness with horses and cattle. Apart from that, they said, she was a fine-looking young woman, albeit a little schoolmistress-like with her gold-rimmed spectacles. Mother never would be a countrywoman, but she came to love grey Galloway as my father loved it, and, in due course, as I loved it myself.

3

Kith and Kin

The poet of my childhood was Robert Burns. It could hardly
have been otherwise, for Burns was as much revered in Galloway
as anywhere in Scotland and nowhere was he quoted more. It
was small wonder that I was soon familiar with his most-quoted
verses - with the result that in later life I never appreciated them
as I might otherwise have done! When I discovered Tennyson I
was inclined to be bored by most of his work, save some of his
pastoral lines such as his reference to 'long fields of barley and
of rye' in 'The Lady of Shalott', and then I found a particular
verse from Will Waterproof's Lyrical Monologue :

> The cock was of a larger egg
> Than modern poultry drop,
> Stept forward on a firmer leg,
> And cramm'd a plumper crop;
> Upon an ampler dunghill trod,
> Crow'd lustier late and early,
> Sipt wine from silver, praising God,
> And raked in golden barley.

There may have been very little wine sipt from silver in my
grandfather's house but somehow those lines of Tennyson's fit
the sort of image I have of my kith and kin. They were all of a
larger egg, it seems to me now, and crow'd lustier late and early.
Every one of them, male or female was what some people would
call a character - bigger, louder, stronger, more fey, more
whimsical and more alive than most. I came into the household
so young and so small that I can't pretend to remember it as it
must have been when my mother and father took their rueful
farewell of me, or say when it was that I was first aware that I

was an important member of the family, to be shown off, admired, weighed, measured and compared with the offspring of relatives outside the direct line of sons of the eldest sons of eldest sons.

My great-grandfather was still alive. He lived to a great age. He was an eldest son, I believe - the somewhat battered family tree eludes me at the moment - and my grandfather was his eldest son. Father was an only son and I was his first son. It was imperative that we should all be assembled before it was too late so that we could have a 'four-generation' picture taken. This was done in due course when I stood on my own feet, sheltered by the Gladstonian figure of my whiskered great-grandfather with the other two generations suitably placed near the patriarch. The old fellow lived with his second son, Charlie, a burly, kind, big-hearted man who farmed some miles away. I won Great-Grandfather's approbation early on. He suffered from chronic deafness and my voice was of a pitch that he could hear. Everyone else had to shout for all they were worth.

There were always relatives coming and going on different days of the week and at different hours of the day, or so it seems to me when nostalgia takes me back, at the drop of a hat, to sit on a cushion on the box-bed settle and enjoy listening to their talk, although most of it was so far above my head that I hardly ever got the gist of anything. The result was that some extraordinary 'facts' remain with me. Great-Grandfather had been a strong man and Grandfather and his brothers were men of remarkable physique, but I had had an ancestor who would get off his pony when the poor beast grew weary and carry it uphill! Great-Great-Grandmother was no ordinary woman either. She hadn't been content to be more than six feet tall but she had to have red hair and be doublejointed! Nannie Callie, she was, and for good measure she was a witch. There must have been some truth in the thing. 'Callie', or 'calzie', is the word for witch and there she is on the family tree along with a few other legendary kinfolk. One of these was hanged for his religion in the days of the Covenant and left a more quick-witted brother who escaped by telling the dragoons, who asked for him by name when they

Four generations of eldest sons: the author John McNeillie
with his great-grand father John McNeillie (left),
his father Robert McNeillie
and his grandfather John McNeillie

met him on the road, that if they hurried they would take 'him' for 'the man they were after' had been there at home until he left!

Like many large country families there were relatives who had the same name: thus we had Wee Johnnie from Sorbie and Wee Johnnie from Wigtown, Auld John and Young John from Sorbie. Much the same applied to Peters, Charlies, Willies and the rest. There was a legion of us and I represented the future as Great-Grandfather represented contact with relatives long laid in the churchyard. Among these, celebrated not by his ability to carry a pony uphill, or cast spells to stop milk churning, was my great-grandfather's great-grandfather to whom my grandfather had talked when the old fellow was 108 years old. He had been what they called a 'rush candle scholar' and whenever any sort of broadsheet or pamphlet filtered through to that remote countryside people would assemble to have the thing read to them by 'the scholar'. And, it was often emphasized, I was a child who should have been born to see my ancestors, if this could have somehow been contrived, for I had in me some extraordinary blood!

There had been, for instance, the ne'er-do-well father of my great-grandfather, or was it his grandfather? A man who could never keep a penny in his pocket if there was an alehouse within a day's travel. Slowly and surely he had consumed his substance as he travelled the primrose-strewn path. Creditors besieged him until he couldn't go to market or sell any of the produce of his farm anywhere inside Galloway. Before Michaelmas he conceived a plan to beat his creditors and bring a few shillings home to brighten life for his wife and children. By night, and by stealth, he prepared a wagon into which he crammed a·large flock of geese and enough meal to feed them until he reached his destination. A net kept the geese from escaping and the wagon set off with Great-Grandfather's father, or grandfather, full of confidence in himself and the success of his plan. The creditors hammered on his door but he wasn't at home. His loyal wife could give no news of him and indeed in the days that followed, while he journeyed across Dumfriesshire, she had none to give. In due course, sufficiently far away from home to offer his geese in the market - one flight of fancy had it that he went all the way down through Carlisle and Westmorland to sell his geese in Liverpool - the purpose of the great expedition was at last realized.

The wagon was turned about and headed for home. There were one or two stops on the way, of course. The roads were long and dusty and a man's throat gets dry. By a sad mischance the money for the geese passed over the alehouse counter in this little place and that until it was all gone! There was, however, an asset that a duller man might have overlooked. The wagon was worth a sovereign or two, and the horse could be ridden. This was done, but by an even sadder mischance the money for the wagon, too, passed into the hands of the publicans (if not the thieves) who drank in the poor fellow's company. Who could blame him for selling the horse and making the final stage of the journey home on foot? Who could blame him for buying a dram here and a dram there, when his misfortunes were so hard to bear? His creditors were upon him when he reached home penniless, and in a short time his farm was sold up.

Well, if it didn't happen I heard it told with a wonderful resemblance to the truth. I was small and the atmosphere of the kitchen with its salt ham hanging from the ceiling, the cats snoozing in the hearth and the iron kettle singing on the big, burnished range, was as heady to me as the malting-floor of the distillery and the fume of spirits was to some of my kin.

'Boy, d'ye ken what I'm going to tell ye?' one would begin. My eyes would grow large with wonder and I would listen to stories of the world not as it was, or had been, perhaps, but as it should have been, with everything in sharp contrast, comedy and tragedy, joy and despair. Now and again someone would shake his head and remark on the things I was learning about people and the world. I would grow up old fashioned, they would swear, and my head would be full of nonsense, which was probably true. To counteract this, Grandfather would read to me from *The Scottish Farmer*. There was nothing like a bit of news on the latest method of treating footrot in black-faced sheep to adjust any tendency to attach too much importance to old men's tales.

'Pay you heed to this, son,' he would say. They had measured me up to be a farmer one day. It was the only thing for a self respecting man to do with his life, an elemental business, ploughing a furrow, scattering corn and, in due time, harvesting tenfold. It was all in the Bible. When *The Scottish Farmer* was exhausted I would be read a passage from the Bible. A respect for religion was also of prime importance. Part of that respect entailed having my corn-coloured girlish locks combed and brushed when the priest arrived on the scene. Grandfather, who was a staunch protestant, had nevertheless contrived to make a close friend of the parish priest. Father Clark was respected as much as the minister and, I think, loved a great deal more and I can't think that any of the family, even those outside the immediate household, ever thought there was anything odd or un-protestant about it.

There were times when kinfolk crowded in upon us and there weren't enough chairs, stools, forms or settles to go round and I would eat my supper perched on my grandfather's knee. I had left my mother a child with a great facility for bringing up his food, but that weakness was soon overcome. How I managed to compete in devouring mounds of oven scones spread with heather honey on top of fresh butter I don't know. 'Pass the cream and give Wee John another bit of shortbread for he looks hungry. . . . Pass the shortbread and give the wee boy some cream. . . .

How was I shaping up? Was I putting good meat on my frame and making good bone? Who could judge better than relatives who knew how to rear the very finest bullocks, bred good Clydesdale horses, won prizes at the cattle shows and never got anything but the top price in the mart? I belonged to the family. I was one of them, and it is hard to explain just what this means in the present generation when families are nothing like as close knit as they once were. My elders looked at me with a special warmth. They sighed and wondered aloud what so-and-so would have thought of me had he lived, for was I not the image of this one or that one, and indisputably 'one of ours'? What my poor mother might have made of this I don't know! I was like my grandfather and I 'took after' Great-Grandfather, and there was a little of Aunt Maggie in me and, dammit, it couldn't be denied that I favoured the best side of the family, the clever ones, the best-looking ones, the strongest, the tallest. One day I would prove it by growing up to be the spitting image of all of them!

It would have been difficult indeed to have grown up in the image of both Grandfather and his brothers. Grandfather was the tallest and long in the leg. He had been lame since boyhood when he had broken a leg in the course of demonstrating some athletic feat. His hands were the biggest hands I have seen on any man and his feet weren't exactly small. He had his boots made for him and there was a legend that on one occasion when he sent one of his helpers to bring back new boots ordered from the shoemaker the young fellow made a mistake and called on the cobbler, who also sold boots. 'I have no size twelves,' said the cobbler, handing over a parcel, 'but tell the master this is the best I can do.' Grandfather's sense of humour was hardly up to coping with the offer of two pairs of size six boots!

His brothers, Great-Uncle Charlie and Great-Uncle Peter, who were simply Uncle Charlie and Uncle Peter to me, were cast in a slightly different mould. They were burly men. Peter was something less than six feet in height but had nevertheless been accepted by the London City Police on account of his very fine physique. Their limit in those days was six feet and Uncle Peter was probably the only policeman in that famous picture of the Sidney Street siege who was under regulation size, although I don't suppose Mr Churchill, or Peter the Painter, noticed the fact. Uncle Peter was undoubtedly the most sophisticated member of the family and when he was home on holiday from London he regaled his relatives with accounts of places and sights they could never hope to see. Particular about his neat appearance, on one occasion he found himself without a white collar. Something had gone wrong with his laundry. It may have been that, although shirts and sheets couldn't be bleached whiter anywhere than on the thorn bush, no one in the country was very practised in starching stiff collars. No matter what the reason, Uncle Peter was determined to look his usual neat and tidy, dignified self. He went into the draper's shop and asked for a size eighteen collar, a stiff one. The draper had a sly sense of humour or perhaps he wanted to take down the stranger with the slightly 'English' accent. 'I'm sorry, sir,' he said. 'We get no call for such large stiff collars but my next-door neighbour can surely fix you up.' Polite as always, Uncle Peter thanked him and withdrew. He was well across the threshold of the next-door shop before he sniffed the air and knew the smell of tanned leather. He was in the saddler's shop. The collars were all a little larger than even he could have worn.

Grandfather and Uncle Charlie inevitably met and compared notes at agricultural shows and other country events of importance. The cattle shows took place in summer and one or another of them would be sure to coincide with Uncle Peter's trip home. The brothers had a deep affection for one another and one's success was the delight of the others. It might fall out that Uncle Charlie had won prizes for his Ayrshires or Shorthorns, or Grandfather had been awarded a red ticket for a Clydesdale foal or perhaps won a prize with a trotting-horse at the sports, which almost always wound up the day. The event that produced almost as much excitement as the trottingraces was the tug-of-war competition. Uncle Peter, a fine athlete, knew something about the art of pulling in a tug-of-war. Uncle Charlie could be persuaded to take off his jacket and appear in shirt and breeches as one of Uncle Peter's carefully chosen team. With a little pre-event coaching Uncle Peter's scratch team would challenge all comers. And how they could perform when they settled down and 'took the strain'! If they didn't win at the first pull there was certainly some danger that bloodvessels would be burst or arms pulled out of their sockets.

There were times when, sitting high on Grandfather's shoulder, it seemed to me that stalemate had been reached and sixteen powerful countrymen were about to tear apart a sisal rope of an inch and a half diameter, and then, all at once, as the crowd held its breath and all that could be heard was the bleating of a sheep or the whinnying of a horse, one side or the other would begin to slip. Hundreds of red-faced countrymen would begin to shout 'Heave! Heave! Heave!', the horses would set their ears, the frightened ponies walk sideways and small boys get their toes trodden upon, while the first slipping heel produced collapse and eight men slithered and slid on their backsides across the green trampled grass. If sometimes Uncles Peter and Charlie weren't on the winning side I must confess that I have chosen, consciously or subconsciously, to eliminate the memory. They always won. Looking back it could not have been otherwise. I loved them and they were my idols, and surely there is nothing wrong in that for a child?

The end of the tug-of-war provided an occasion for a special demonstration of physical exhaustion, proving that a man had given all he had and had almost pulled himself to death. Uncle Peter would stand up for a moment and then turn and fall on his back, his arms outstretched and his eyes closed, his chest heaving. The crowd would close in and express their admiration, after which, being the athlete he was, Uncle Peter would recover, put on his jacket, tie his tie and explain how he had whispered advice to his side to hold their effort until the precise moment when they had induced their rivals to fall like ninepins. It always puzzled me that Uncle Peter never fell on his face, but then he was probably too old a hand to do anything so careless. His white shirt front would have been badly stained by the grass. It always did get stained, of course, but never where it would have spoilt his tidy appearance. Every good performer has to be something of a showman!

If I had relatives I hadn't seen for a long time it was at the cattle shows I met them. I think there were some, far-out cousins and the second cousins of far-out cousins, whom I only met at cattle shows, just as there were even more remote kin whose existence I only discovered when there was a death in the family, relatives who were excused attendance at weddings, but had to be there to pay their last respects to the dead. As I have said, the trees were tall and the mornings bright with sunshine. Naturally, I had a great affection for every one of my kith and kin.

4

Horse Sense

My small world, it seems, was dominated by the existence of the horse as the most important animal next to man, with the result that I am moved by the sight of the few great draught horses that have survived to the present day. Horses stood high. The biggest of them had feet far bigger than the biggest plate on the dresser and when a cleg alighted on their bellies they didn't only whisk at it with their tails or stamp on the cobbles angrily but they twitched a muscle, and the pestilential bloodsucker would be persuaded to give up his biting and move elsewhere. This was a thing that I saw and marvelled at when I stood in the hayfield in summer or played in an enclosure of sheaves when the corn was being harvested. Despite the enormous size of the roan mare, who stood eighteen hands high, I wasn't afraid of her. I rode home perched on her neck, jolting and swaying, with my hands entwined in her long mane.

There isn't much room on a horse's neck when the beast is wearing a collar, but I rode there. Something looks after the small and the helpless and saves them from the fate of more nervous individuals of mature age. I had, after all, taken my first faltering steps on the tiled floor of the kitchen, with sleeping dogs lying about and fat, lazy cats squatting like delft ornaments at every turn and corner, to say nothing of the pet hen that picked her way in and out again, ready to fly up and bring the house down if she disturbed one of the dogs. Horse sense is something that a lot of people lack and it was something the family set great store by.

Horses were people of a special sort. Since they couldn't speak they had to be communicated with one way or another and they had to be brought up, as children have to be brought up, to know their duty, their part in the scheme of things. It was carrying it all rather far, perhaps, to have long conversations with Jess, Mary, Jean, Bob, Clyde, Tammy, Prince and Star, to allow them to push their way in at the kitchen door in an attempt to join the family, to feed them scones and jam or bread and butter, according to their taste, and to make as much fuss of them in every other way as ordinary families made of their children, but this is how it was. I sometimes think I should have included horses among my relatives, but then what of the cats, the dogs, the pet lamb, the favourite white-faced calf, and old Johnnie the bull who stood to have his head scratched and his maleness made nonsense of by the use of pet-names and pretty words?

When it came to adjusting this relationship and putting things in proper perspective the butcher was summoned to kill the pampered pig, and Stewart, horse-dealer, horse-doctor and acknowledged expert, came to correct some fault in the young horse or put the mare through her paces in readiness for the show. No one had more horse sense than Stewart. He could make an old horse look young, a horse that threw out a foot as it walked look as though it had a perfect gait. There was nothing he didn't know about horses but he didn't talk to them. His communication with horses was a sort of telepathy. He took the bridle in his hand and the animal knew him!

Send for Stewart, they would say. He'll soon put it right. He knows whether she stands a chance in the ring. He'll show Jeck how to walk her round, how to soap her hocks and curry her back the right way. Send for Stewart and Grandfather would in due course send word to his farm. Would Stewart come and look at the horse and give his opinion?

It was something more than a G.P. calling in a specialist. Everyone waited for Stewart to come. He was, of course, a blood relation. I was never quite sure where he came in but he belonged on Grandfather's side of the family and was, I think, a second cousin to my father. If I am wrong I hope he won't come back from the horse fairs and dealers' rings of his particular heaven to reproach me with any mistake I may have made in our relationship. Like all the horse-dealers and horse-breakers of that time, Stewart dressed in loud checks. His trousers were tight-legged and as often as not he wore brown boots, and cap or bowler at a jaunty angle. His step was light and his eye as keen and sharp as the crow. When I think of him now he reminds me of a well-worn, polished hazel stick. His voice was loud and harsh and he had a way of saying outrageous things that startled and sometimes offended his more sensitive listeners. He had been educated in a hard school, made bargains with crafty horse-dealers in Galloway and across the water in Ireland. His alertness was all-important to his survival. Nothing in the business was ever quite what it seemed and a bargain was only a bargain after the froth had been blown or wiped away! The sovereigns that found their way into his purse were earned with no less effort than the ploughman earned his wages turning a furrow in a field long lying fallow.

When Stewart came he enlivened the household with his racy stories of the countryside. His laugh was hearty. He was a bachelor at that time, although he married later in life, and his house was looked after by an elderly and very deaf housekeeper to whom he would make outrageous comments and bawdy suggestions knowing that she could achieve no more than a wild guess at what he said. The answers he obtained were sometimes even more outrageous in their context than the questions put, and of course, they grew with imagination and natural embellishment. Rabelais would surely have taken Stewart to his bosom. I would sit beside him and wonder that a man could laugh so loudly and shock so many of his listeners. Now and again he would catch my eye and then I knew he was like me underneath. The loud voice and the wild jokes were a fence around him. Before he went out to look at the particular animal he had been called upon to vet he would press a sixpence into my hand and whisper to me to put it in my pocket without letting anyone know. This wasn't to encourage me to be cunning and set up a hoard of pennies begged from relatives. He didn't want the world to know that underneath the carved oak of his hard countenance and the façade of the horsedealer, he was kind and gentle. He understood a child as well as he understood horses.

'We can make the best of her,' he would say, 'she being a carnapcious* misbegotten creature, if we hold her head in and walk her round, so that she turns her arse-end out all the time. Then, if they ask for her to be brought back, Jeck can take her a wee bit faster the second time and they won't see how she throws her foot, d'ye see what I mean?'

The demonstration would produce a gasp of admiration. All it needed to ensure success was for Stewart himself to lead the mare at the show, but there were rules and regulations about this kind of thing and it was well known that experts could make silk purses out of sows' ears! Stewart would coach the ploughman or whatever member of the immediate family was to 'show' the mare, and when he had done so the chances of winning were considerably enhanced. The task done, he would return to the house to be regaled with the finest supper the kitchen could produce and perhaps he and Grandfather would take a dram. Long past my bedtime, I would sit there and listen to stories of bad horses and crooked dealers and the dodges of a business in which only the fittest could survive. Did they file a mare's teeth to disguise her age? Certainly they did, but not to fool the expert! They trimmed and oiled the hooves, soaped and curried the animal wherever an outline had to be obscured, and, it was whispered, fed the hollow-bellied creature a mash containing lead shot to fill it out, and sometimes caned the beast's back to make it swell- but not to deceive men born with horse sense. These were the tricks of the fellows who thought themselves cunning in the world of horse-dealing. The expert looked at the horse's eye and knew its age before he opened its mouth. He ran his hands gently over its back and its hocks and its belly and said nothing. He took the bridle in his own hand and walked it a pace or two without guiding it. When he had done that he had blown the froth away and knew more about the dealer than was revealed when he looked him in the face. Stewart had seen it all. I am afraid that outside his own kin he trusted no one.

* *Carnapcious - awkward, difficult, contrary.*

There were times of course when Stewart came unsummoned. His farm was no more than six or seven miles away and his bachelor existence had to be relieved by purely social contact. He was always warmly welcomed by Grandmother who, I think, understood the gentleness that underlay his apparent hardness. The talk was invariably of horses and cattle of one sort or another. If the weather was at all anything like, we would all be out at the fence, myself hoisted on someone's shoulder, or carried in the crook of Grandfather's arm, so that the pony could be studied, the foal admired, and its good or bad points gone over in preparation for a show or the ring at the mart. What Stewart said was as important as a pronouncement from the pulpit for it wasn't every family that had such an expert judge of horseflesh to consult.

Not unnaturally, the horses lived a lifetime with us. Jean, the brood mare, was a young mare when I was a small child and I grew up with her. Tammy, the trottingpony, was barely a year older than I was, and Bob only a year or two older. Somewhere along the way we lost old Jess and there was more than one Mary. If there was a horse with character, and horses like dogs often grow to be like their masters, it was Bob, old blind-of an-eye Bob, the Irish rig with the mahogany dapples on his rotund body. Bob grew to be one of the family more than any other horse. His sense of humour was distinct. He would flick an ear and then quickly move his head and take all the buttons off the overcoat of someone leading him to the stable or backing him into a gig. The buttons tumbled, the coat fell open. It was all over in an instant and the horse would be standing contemplatively looking down at the road. My brother once plagued old Bob overmuch by running under his belly and generally making a nuisance of himself until the horse turned and caught him by the hair and kept him standing on tiptoe and crying for all he was worth until help came. The same old codger had a cunning way of keeping the trace chains taut when he was hitched in front to help haul a load of dung up a steep hill, but he could be caught out by anyone who knew him well. A walking-stick laid on the

"Old Bob" the Irish rig; he liked to remove buttons and pretend to work!

chain would make it sag. Old Bob would show the white of one eye and throw himself into his collar to pull his weight until he thought it safe to swing the lead once again.

There was a day of drama in my young life when Bob almost lost his life. Corn was being carted from the face of the big hill, the high-built cart traversing the brow and gathering in the last few stooks on that dangerous slope, when all at once the cart overturned. The sheaves cascaded downhill, the uppermost wheel spun for a minute or two and was still. Far across the field the harvesters stopped and stared. The collie dog cocked his ears. Everyone on the golden hill was motionless and silent and then the dog began to run, barking with the excitement. I remember a hare rising from the stubble and going frantically away uphill and putting a covey of partridges to flight as it ran through them. Grandfather started to run as fast as his lame leg would let him. The harvesters cried out in alarm. They knew that the weight of the horse's body would hang it in its collar, for the collar was linked to the shafts by the hames. It was a thing that happened quickly. A horse gave a kick or two and then thrashed and struggled and that was it. I was too young to know what the alarm meant, but I ran too, the sharp stubbles stinging the soles of my feet, for I was always barefoot at that time. Soon I was close enough to see Bob. He was lying blind-side down and Grandfather knelt at his head.

'Lie still, Bob,' he said. 'Lie still now and don't kick!'

Bob didn't move while his master fumbled in his waistcoat pocket for the sharp knife he used to pare his tobacco twist. It took only a minute to open the knife and cut the leather strap that linked the hames and when the hames slid away from the collar the pressure on Bob's neck was relieved.

'Canny now,' said Grandfather as he pulled the cart saddle strap and released the buckle. 'Canny,' he said again as he reached for the breeching-chains and pulled them clear of the shafts. It was a tricky and dangerous operation, for if the horse had taken fright he could easily have inflicted a serious injury upon anyone trying to free him, but at last he was free.

'Come away now and throw back the sheaves,' Grandfather called to the men. The sheaves were thrown back with great speed and when this was done Grandfather lay down with his arm across the horse's neck, talking to him quietly while the cart was dragged back and finally manhandled clear.

'There ye are now, Bob,' said Grandfather. 'Up on your feet and we'll see if you are any the worse.'

Bob got to his feet and shook his head, making the collar swing. He shivered just once and then began to crop the oats from one of the near-at-hand sheaves. No one stopped him. Everyone was relieved that he had suffered no injury. Only the Irish harvesters hurried to resume work. They were on contract and couldn't be expected to understand that a member of the family had had a narrow escape!

When the story of Bob's accident was told afterwards, as it often was, Grandfather would stress the importance of talking to horses and achieving an understanding with them. The trouble with most people, he would say, was that they couldn't appreciate that although a horse couldn't talk back it could think and understand. It was capable of reasoning things out and the man who marked the horse down as a dumb and therefore stupid sort of beast was ignorant and stupid himself.

Bob certainly proved that he could work out problems on an occasion when he was yoked to the gig and took Grandfather into town one evening to meet some friends. They dallied rather long in the Galloway Arms, and when Grandfather emerged at last and toddled round to the mews to light the gig lamps and set Bob on the road for home, he was more than a little the worse for wear. The travelling-rugs became entangled round his feet; the reins, too, had a tendency to get crossed; and it was only with difficulty that the wheels cleared the walls on the cobbled pathway from the mews to the square. It was a frosty night. The stars were far up and small. The square was deserted. The last of the lights along the lower street had gone out and black cats ran hurriedly from one pool of darkness to the next. It was no wonder that Grandfather decided that the frost and cold could the better be avoided down in the well of the gig where the travellingrugs had tumbled. He allowed himself to settle down, ever so gently, and Bob plodded down the steep hill and on along the silent road, through the overhanging ash and elm trees and over the bridge, home. It was a journey that required no more than a homing instinct and Bob had that. Most horses have it, but when he turned off the public road there were three gates to be negotiated. The first one opened inwards and was held by a wire loop. Bob backed a little way and sidled up to the gate so that he could lift the loop with his teeth. After this he pushed his way through and the cart threw the gate back. Two hundred yards farther up the rough road was the second gate which opened outwards. A chain held this one. Bob lifted the chain with his teeth and backed away to open the gate. But when he reached the third and last gate, which opened inwards and wasn't fastened by wire or chain, he found that he couldn't force it back because it wouldn't clear the road. There he was, perhaps a hundred yards from home, with Grandfather sound asleep in the well of the trap! A less intelligent animal would have waited until help came, but Bob turned round and went back to the second gate and then walked up the field until he came opposite the house where the gig lamps could be seen and help summoned.

Grandfather was home and dry, or as dry as a man can be when he has had one dram too many. The family blessed old Bob and gave him a special mash. Next day he had two or three buttered crusts while he stood waiting for the milk to be loaded on the spring cart. I am sure he knew why. Grandfather talked to him and explained about the frosty night and the effects of whisky when it was very cold. Bob knew the smell of whisky and how it made a man fuddled, just as I already knew about these things, although on this occasion I slept through the vigil and the minor drama of Grandfather's late return from the town.

5

Sunday on the Shore

There must have been a particular instant when the idea of a picnic on the shore took hold in someone's imagination. I think it happened in the very early morning at that hopeful time when a radiance from the sun comes spreading up from behind the Galloway hills, beyond the undulating farmland and the mist-clothed hollows and the river estuary. The most hopeful time of the day is surely when the day begins, when day comes like a great forest fire taking hold, in a blaze of red and gold shading to a mellow yellowness. Mornings were quiet save for a bird calling somewhere out in the moss or a beast lowing in the pasture. Whoever rose to start the day, to fan the embers of the almost dead fire with a folded newspaper, set the kettle to boil and draw water from the pump, looked to the east and thought the world was wonderful. So it was. It was never more wonderful except perhaps when there was no day of work to be faced and morning grew into noon and we were all enjoying a life of ease, off by the sea. The marvel of the new day might have tarnished a little by the time the family were all hurrying about, when milking-pails were rattling and churns being rolled and horses were led by the forelock down from the dew-drenched field.

'We'll go to the shore on Sunday. What do you think?' someone would say. 'If Father says the weather will stay.' The sun would break from the sheltering hills to bathe fields of swedes and white- and purple-blossomed potato fields in its magic light. Whoever had the inspiration would stand and stare at the barley and oats, the broad acres of dairy pasture, and admire the silhouetted trees and the endless, snaking drystone walls and repeat, 'On Sunday we'll picnic on the shore.'

When Grandfather came back from his creamery run he would

drop the reins and let someone else unyoke the horse from the spring cart. He, too, had looked at the sun, listened to the cocks crowing, heard the curlew crying and was intoxicated by the air of the morning. He was ready for his breakfast, ready to trim the crust from his bread and dip it in the yolk of his soft-boiled egg, talk of so-and-so's corn that was spattered by thistles or a turnip field devastated by crows until it looked like an old moth-eaten rug. 'We were thinking, Father,' one of my aunts would say, 'that we might take a picnic on the shore on Sunday.' And the die was cast.

'Ah well,' Grandfather would say. 'Just so. The weather will last six or seven days. I timed the carry last night.'

The 'carry' was a high clear space in the far-up clouds.

It was something that only the weather-wise knew about. It was hard to recognize and distinguish from any other clear space in the heavens but it was there, and from the time it appeared to the time the heavens closed in had great bearing on the duration of dry spells. Even so, this evening study of the heavens had to be checked against the morning's light. When he had finished his breakfast Grandfather would go out and make a second appraisal of the weather signs.

It was like waiting for a judge to pass judgement or a doctor to complete his diagnosis and I am sure Grandfather knew how everyone hung on his words. A prophet must never be denied his moments of glory.

'It will be a fine day on Sunday,' he would promise and from that moment whoever had thought of Sunday on the shore would think of nothing else until the picnic was over. It would be a family picnic, of course, and cousins from Sorbie would come. Uncle Charlie would be persuaded to show his face if this could be contrived, but not until he had done his duty as an elder in the kirk. If time or circumstances prevented relatives from joining in there was still the joiner's daughter at the road-end and perhaps the blacksmith's daughter, Bella, would like to come. They, of course, would ride on bicycles and some of the family would do so too, for there was only so much room in the gig. The gig would be crammed with baskets and teapots and kettles, the fire-blackened utensils hurriedly wrapped in newspaper lest they blacken dresses. The baskets of food would be held by anyone and everyone. Even Grandfather might balance one with his right hand and hold the reins with his left. Food would be ample for the hungriest appetite that the sea-air could induce: soda scones and pancakes plastered with salt butter and gooseberry jam, tins of home-made shortbread, a fat cream cake that even when cut would prove too thick for the biggest mouth, biscuits, oatcakes, oatmeal scones, treacle scones and oven scones. All this and a bag of oats for the pony and a pail to carry water from the well.

To complete the arrangements they worked harder in the kitchen than they did even at the height of harvest or on a threshing-day. Everything had to be just perfect. There were only so many glorious Sundays in a summer, so many sun-drenched mornings and wonderful hot and drowsy afternoons. The older ones knew there were only so many of these in a lifetime and no one could afford to squander a single one or allow anything to mar it. Only the collie dog was unaffected by the excitement. I think he always sensed what was happening in the uncanny way that dogs do and knew that he would be left to guard the empty house. He brooded more and more as Sunday approached, poor creature. Perhaps at the last minute the ploughman would put off his visit to his relatives and stay with the dog but everyone else lived for the day on the shore and no one would miss it for anything. 'Have you forgotten?' one would light-heartedly ask another during the days that followed. 'We're off to the shore on Sunday!' But who could have forgotten when no one talked of anything else or thought of anything but the picnic, the crabs and limpets we would bring back, the whiskered codfish Grandfather would buy from the fisherman who lived in the cottage along the shore, if he had been out with his boat the day before.

Ordinarily Sundays went at a leisurely pace. No one wondered about the spring cart's late return or fretted if breakfast was disorganized by a general lack of haste. There was no great

41

anxiety if the sun plunged suddenly into a cloud or shadows like giant sheep ran across the distant hills. No one went to the fence to see if the Atlantic mist was crawling up to mar the day. They plodded on with their morning chores for a change in the light threatened no one's dreams and no harvesting or any other everyday task was done on Sunday. The flock of Leghorns and black Minorcas were fed because they had to be fed. Skim milk was poured into pig troughs and someone plied the byre brush and ran the barrow on to the midden after the byre walks were cleaned. A shore Sunday was different. Hurry, hurry, they urged one another, scald the churns and have the driver's breakfast ready while you debate the need for waterproof coats. The merest suggestion of a shadow on the window made one or another of the family run out to check on the weather again. If the bees were still buzzing round the hives and the hens dust-bathing under the flowering currant and the cock crowing, God was in His heaven.

The light-hearted and least burdened members of the family were those who could travel unencumbered, riding on a bicycle. They could set out before the rest, trundling through the puddles of the old road, swaying and wobbling and laughing until they were lost to view beyond the march gate - the gate through the boundary of the farm. The vanguard were usually seen no more until the gig came down the long hill to the shore, the moorland journey over and its destination in sight.

I went on these picnics when I was a toddler and longed to travel with the carefree ones who went on ahead, but my place was in the gig until I was old enough to straddle a bicycle, and what better place to travel, I wonder now. I could see beyond the drystone walls, bracken banks and hillocks of bilberry to the clumps of trees on the skyline and the moorfarms huddling in sheltered places, peaceful, shut-away little whitewashed steadings that slept in a haze of summer heat. I loved to watch the black-faced sheep and the shaggy bullocks that grazed on the wild moss and the rabbits that bobbed in their hundreds across acres of short springy turf that had never known the plough. To tell the truth I could never bear waiting for the journey to begin and was only content when we followed the bicycle contingent down the road where I looked for signs of their passing, the brown cloud of mud in a puddle and the print of a bicycle tyre on a big flat stone. I never looked back. I looked ahead for the tunnel of the old ash trees, the solitary hawthorn, the derelict and broken-down cothouse (all farm cottages were known as cothouses in that part of the country), landmarks on the road to the shore which the pony travelled at an unhurried trot, the harness jingling and a hollow rumbling coming from the well of the gig where crockery jostled against cutlery and those teapots and kettles wrapped in newspaper. Thinking of it now I see the cloudless sky, the shimmering landscape, the sun high. If the stones of the wall were ever damp with moisture from a summer shower I never noticed, nor heard the faintest sound of distant thunder. The grasshoppers sang in the verges, adders basked, adders that couldn't hear a footfall and loved the stones and the hot sun. The leaves of the rowan tree fluttered gently in a breeze that cooled our cheeks.

The journey took us across the moor, through firplantings, up the grey road to the country schoolhouse, which stood in isolation behind a more solidly built drystone wall than those that divided adjoining fields, and over a rise to the deciduous trees that were commoner than pines and larches in the woods above the shore. The cottagers' dogs barked as we passed and hens scampered in front of the wheels of the gig while the children of the little stone houses stared at us or shyly waved a greeting, but our thoughts were elsewhere. We were eager for the first glimpse of the sea. We could already hear it and smell the seaweed, or so we fancied, when we still had a mile or so to go. The pony quickened his pace as he went downhill. He, too, knew we were near the sea and the end of our journey.

'The sea! The sea!' we cried and there it was, a pale blue haze between the fluttering foliage of the trees, as blue as the soft blue of the sky and almost indistinguishable from it. The shafts of the gig were down and the pony's heels slipped now and again. One or two of us would have to get out and walk that the gig might arrive without serious mishap but no one minded walking when we were all but there.

Where were the cyclists? They were generally at the iron gate leading down to the shore and the long disused fisherman's cottage that provided a picnic shelter. Sometimes they were on the tideline gathering driftwood for the fire. Sometimes they had a fire already kindled in the shelter of the cottage walls for the ruin had long since lost its roof and timbers, but more often than not they stood waiting for us and we all went down together, greeting one another and our relatives from Sorbie, bumping and jolting and swaying, laughing and talking and full of excitement, for the seaside atmosphere, the smell of the seaweed, the cry of the seabirds, the sunlight and the wonderful peace of the place transported our spirits. 'Watch for adders!' someone would shout but the adder that filled us with horror in the hayfield had no terror for us here and somehow always hurried from our path to glide into the stunted bracken and the low creeping blackberry bushes that clothed boulders looking like sleeping pigs. In a little while we would all be enjoying ourselves, picking up coloured shells and bits of sun-hardened seaweed, exploring the rocks, flushing rock doves from their nesting-ledges and walking on and on, far out of earshot of our elders who busied themselves about the picnic fire, laying down travelling-rugs, brushing away the fragments of weed and sand and grit, and trying to make themselves comfortable so that they could doze in the soporific atmosphere about the old cottage at the top of the shingle.

Grandfather liked to sit and smoke his pipe, recalling how he had come to the very stone he was sitting upon when a small boy. The place hadn't changed in a lifetime and never would it seemed, for who would want to change those little fields above the shore where potatoes grew among the stones with only a handful of soil to nourish them? Who could live in such a place but a man who knew how because he had been bred in it, a peasant born of peasants? After a while Grandfather would take his customary walk along the tideline and struggle through the rocks so that he could move a few polished boulders in the pools and gather crabs that lived under the beards of weed. He was fond of crabs and liked to knock limpets off the rocks, for these were tasty when taken home and 'cleaned' and boiled like mussels. The absorbing business of collecting red crabs or robbing the rock doves would come to an end when someone back at the ruined cottage beat upon an old can or a tin tray with a piece of driftwood, sounding the call to the feast; and back we would swarm, the largest and the smallest of us, each at his own best pace, to eat our fill of salt beef, roast chicken, apple tart, red cheese or whatever else had been brought to restore our flagging energy. Eating at a picnic was as much a point of honour as it was when visiting friends. It was the pride of my aunts that no matter what the appetites of those who sat down to the picnic might be they would have enough. It would have been wasteful to have left anything! The mounds of scone and jam were demolished. The pancakes were bolted down. The shortbread done justice to because it was the best shortbread anyone had ever tasted and the sponge cake too. When eating was at an end and the black iron teapot had been emptied once and sometimes refilled and emptied again it was time to bathe our feet, to wade in the pools and meet the waves rolling in. The sea was never warm enough to make bathing entirely pleasant. It came in cold deep currents from the Mull of Galloway and rolled up the shore, churning the pebbles but never getting warm enough not to shock anyone who swam to meet it. There were no great swimmers among us. A ducking in the sea was good for children. Their elders felt better for contact with salt water and hobbled painfully through the shingle to wet their feet then hobbled back again. Salt water and salt air cured many things, real and imagined.

Perhaps when we were sporting ourselves away along the shore or while some of us were dozing on the travelling-rugs someone might set the kettle to boil again and there would be a sort of revival of the picnic to finish off an apple tart or some other sweet delight that had been specially hoarded for the purpose, but sometimes the fire had died and the kettle stopped singing among the blackened stones and the whole world dozed for a while, drugged by the air, falling asleep with hats over their eyes. The sleepers missed the cormorants flighting up the bay and didn't hear the clamour of the newly arrived oyster-catchers as they hurried to search along the tideline debris. There is a time in the day at such a place, when, without a clock or anything to mark the hour, a subtle change takes place. All at once afternoon runs to evening. The note of the seabirds seems to change and the sound of the waves too. Grandfather would arise and look at the rocks and without taking out his fat watch, would say that it was time those who were to be back for the milking were on their way. If a smoky cup of tea happened to be on hand he would have it and a bite to eat but after that we must gather ourselves and get ready for the road, taking with us the souvenirs from the seaweed tangles, crabs, limpets and codfish bought from the fisherman.

There was almost as much excitement in the preparation for departure as there had been at the beginning of the day. We shouted to hear our voices echoed in the caves. We hurried back to the water to throw yet another great ostrich egg of a pebble into the waves and came running to the gig to stow aboard some special treasure we had found. Now the pots and crocks were less carefully wrapped and we were more hilarious than ever so that the pony cocked his ears and moved nervously in the shafts, and it was hard to get into the gig when he was eager to leave a place that had changed us all into noisy, carefree wild creatures. Back we went along the moorland road, stopping in the glow of the setting sun to pick a dish of bilberries from the bank if the berries weren't too hard to be cooked in a pie. The cothouse children stared at us again the way they might have stared at a company of merry drinkers, and to tell the truth we were drunk with all we had done and seen, drunk with the sunshine and the clean, fresh air from away beyond the Mull. We sang Harry Lauder's favourite song, 'Keep Right on to the End of the Road', and all the world knew we had been on a picnic, the startled grouse, the astonished sheep, the keeper in his lodge among the trees. Sometimes I looked back and screwed up my eyes to get rid of tears for when the world is so wonderful a child sometimes cannot quite bear it all and must cry a little. The day should have gone on forever but sometimes my intoxication overcame me completely and I fell asleep breathing the scent of woodsmoke, firwoods, honeysuckle, meadowsweet and I didn't even awaken when they carried me in and laid me on the settle.

6

Milk and Honey

The biblical description of a land flowing with milk and honey took my imagination from the moment I first heard it. It seemed to me that I lived in this land, and in a way I did, for I was well used to the sight of great bowls of cream skimmed from the milk to make butter, to the very smell of milk and the intestinal rumblings of ruminating cows waiting to be hurried down the road to the pasture when milking was over, and to the scent and taste of honey. Milk and honey are two of the oldest harvests of man, sweet, rich and natural. Samson fed on honey and look what he did with the jawbone of an ass!

Grandfather had great faith in honey and knew that it had great health-giving benefits for those who spread it on their bread. He had a sweet tooth himself, despite the fact that he smoked a hard black twist that could only be cut with the sharpest knife and rendered smoke-worthy after perhaps an hour's rubbing in the palm. He took honey with his bread after breakfast and honey on his 'piece' in the field, even if no one else did. I believe he knew which lot of bees had gathered the honey he tasted and he would talk about special years the way a connoisseur of wines talks of vintages. It was, after all, the same thing. When the clover was rich and there was an abundance of blossom on the fields during the months when the heather was budding and growing to bloom again, honey was plentiful. It was also affected by the particular sorts of flowers that were at hand in great profusion as a result of favourable conditions in a particular month. Rain and drought, or late frost, affected the 'blend' of the honey stored in the hive. Each harvest was unrepeatable. It could never be exactly the same as the year before, or any year that would ever come again, for hours of sunshine, days of mist or rain, humidity or the cooler wind from the north, all contributed.

The honey we put on our bread could never be successfully separated from the comb. We were too near the moss and the heather banks for that. If the early gathering contained a fair proportion of clover the chances were that bees overlaid it with heather honey. No one minded. The hives were equipped with sections and not with the much larger frames, which, from the point of view of economy, are far less wasteful, since once the honey has been extracted or spun, they can be put back to give the bees less work in cell-building. We ate heather honey as most people eat it, spreading wax and honey on to our bread. We used it to ease a sore throat or cure the 'hoast'. Many a night, when I had been fast asleep but disturbing others with a tickling cough, I was rudely awakened to be told I must take a spoonful of heather honey that all but filled my mouth!

The bees had always been with us, it seemed. They were certainly there before I arrived on the scene and descendants of the original strain remained until Grandfather died. They might have been handed down in the family, but my father didn't take up beekeeping on his own account until some time after his father died. Many a family keeps bees without being aware of them except on those occasions when they go to rob them of their honey, or bribe them with a little sugar candy, but not our family. The bees, like every other living thing with which we were involved, were part of the household, important to us, or at least important to Grandfather who would 'hap' them up in blankets for the winter, move them about, turn them away from the rain if he had to, study the dead they carried out and watch their minor clashes with their enemies. It annoyed him to see a sow rubbing herself on a post that fenced the bees in their particular corner of the old stackyard field. He watched how the pullets came close under the front boards of the hives to pick up the things the bees had cleared from the hive, a dead fly, a moth encased in wax or the eggs of some parasite that had had the temerity to come in and try to share their comfortable quarters.

When he wasn't working at some paper plan for a modification to his machinery or implements, Grandfather was usually studying the bees. When the mood took him he would pick up his stick and tramp up to the angle of the drystone wall and the thorn hedge that enclosed the kitchen garden and take the lid off one of the hives so that he could study how they were doing. He only did this on balmy days and he rarely protected his hands or face. Bees, however, are inclined to be like their owners. A quick-tempered, impatient man will have at least one colony that has his own characteristics. Grandfather had his 'bad' bees, black bees that always fought grimly and resented the slightest intrusion upon their privacy. It was said that his worst brood of bees never swarmed but killed off the old queen without swarming and the colony became stronger and more ill-tempered year by year. Whether this was true or not, the remaining colonies would swarm when conditions were suitable.

Grandfather was never far out in his estimates. He would look up at the bee corner and remark that it would be any day now. The bees were beginning to mill around above the hive while inside the major decision, to swarm or not to swarm, was being debated. The debate sometimes went on well past high noon and instead of going out to the field Grandfather would sit and wait for it. All at once the number of bees buzzing and singing above a certain hive would reach an unprecedented density. Grandfather would jump to his feet. 'Dammit to hell, they're off!' he would exclaim like someone at a trotting-race. Woe betide anyone who attempted to slip off round the side of the house on the pretext that she had linen to spread in the sun, or a picking of peas to gather from the garden. Everyone was conscripted at once. 'Haste ye!' was the general cry and one would rush for a bucket of water, another for the syringe. Everyone else would be expected to arm themselves with tin cans and sticks, pots and wooden spoons, for we were a summer thunderstorm, the gentle rain from heaven, that would persuade the swarm to settle immediately in the green sallow tree, or on the first branch that would bear their weight! As though the house were on fire we would clatter down the steps and across the road, through the wooden gate or over the stone stile and up within range of the swarming bees. The spray would fill the air and blow back upon us. No one would hear what his neighbour said for the clashing of tin and the drumming on pots. More water! More noise! The swarm might settle quickly, but more often than not that secret session within the hive had been to decide where they were going. Their destination was generally somewhere beyond the skyline and they would rise and leave us beneath our vapour rainbows. The situation changed immediately this happened. 'Have done!' Grandfather would command at the top of his voice. 'If you had been quicker on the scene and hadn't hung about the kitchen playing with the range we might have stopped them!'

A homemade rainstorm and the roll of thunder behind them only made the bees increase their speed. Soon they would be a small dark cloud trailing away over the field. Grandfather, throwing the syringe down for someone else to retrieve, would take a pace or two and put up a hand to shade his eyes so that he could judge where they might drop. As often as not the young swarm headed for some other beekeeper's ground.

'I wouldn't be surprised if they didn't settle at Willie Skimming's,' Grandfather would remark sorrowfully, 'but if I could come up with them somewhere near the low planting I might get them back yet.'

The family would sigh and hope that Grandfather took a long walk so that they could restore some order to the kitchen, pack away the pots and wooden spoons and take a cup of tea while they recovered from the inspired panic that had held them for perhaps an hour.

Once in a while, when he was very busy in the hayfield, the bees would steal a march on Grandfather. Someone would look out in the middle of a particularly sultry afternoon and see that a swarm was about to go. It became a matter of fine judgement as to when the alarm should be given, for if the bees were sufficiently active before a warning was sent to the hayfield the hullabaloo of potclattering and frantic rain-making would be avoided, even if no one expected to avoid recriminations when it was discovered that a colony had divided and a queen and her followers, worth a load of hay, had taken themselves off halfway across the shire and perhaps out of Galloway altogether!

I remember an occasion when we visited friends on a neighbouring farm and in the course of making a shortcut on the way back we discovered one of our lost swarms. It had established itself inside the rotten trunk of a tall, dead pine tree. Bees were buzzing everywhere and it was apparent that the swarm had inhabited the tree for at least a year. A good quantity of honey might be had if we brought a bucket and an axe. Grandfather was duly informed and could hardly wait to get up to the wood. He identified the swarm by catching a bee and studying it in his fingers. It was one of his, he said. I don't think anyone expected him to say anything but that. With a veil over his head he set about cutting his way into the rotten tree. The bees buzzed around and the shadowed wood became darkened by their numbers. The wood debris flew until Grandfather reached the comb and lifted it out into a can. He found the queen and put her in a small ventilated box which he laid in with the honey and brood comb he had ladled from the tree. I had long since stumbled and scrambled back through the briars and nettles into the shelter of the thick larches. The bees hummed angrily for a long time and then, when most of them layered themselves to protect the imprisoned queen, or to steal back their honey, Grandfather hastened to cover them with a muslin sheet. A considerable swarm followed him through the trees and over the drystone wall as he carried the can back home. One of them stung me on the neck, but that was nothing. Once bees had closed both of my eyes for a day!

I was much more used to the tall tales of my elders than to the world of fairy tales with giants and demons but when Grandfather decided to gather his honey I was all at once in the worst of the Grimms' world. The bees fought as never before and although Grandfather stood his ground and took his due some of his helpers would be put to flight, clawing at bees in their hair and stumbling in search of the blue-bag. I watched the battle from the comparative safety of the kitchen. Grandfather seemed a hundred feet high and the bees as malevolent as any set of demons Messrs Grimm had created. The air was filled with their anger. It infected their neighbours. Calves and pigs that inquisitively ventured too near, attracted perhaps by the assortment of cans and buckets and other pieces of apparatus Grandfather had gathered about him, threw up their heels, bellowed or grunted and went jogging off into the lower boggy regions beneath the elms, a thousand bees persecuting them as they ran, while ten thousand more closed in on the great robber despite his furious efforts to smoke them stupid.

It was when a great load of honey was brought to the kitchen in a sort of running battle that my comparative safety was seriously impaired. Some of the bees followed the sections of honey right into the house, down the corridor and through to the front porch and nothing would get them out. It would be nightfall, perhaps, before the remaining warriors re-entered their plundered castle and the browsing calves could venture back to graze within a few feet of the rail fence that enclosed the hives. We had more honey than any ordinary family might have consumed in a year, but no matter, years of plenty were to be followed by years of famine, the good book said. The undamaged sections were stored where even the most venturesome mouse couldn't sample the wax and let the sweet contents of the comb run out. Damaged sections were stood on saucers and the honey that leaked was used to sweeten scones and cakes. By the time the corn harvest was in, the honey store was more or less in order. Grandfather was out of the porch and Grandmother could move in to make mushroom ketchup or blackberry wine, or leave a jelly bag straining when she was making apple jelly or jelly from the rowans that grew in profusion along the road to the peat moss.

Most of the honey was consumed by the family but now and again a friend or relative would be given a present of a particularly perfect section. There is something very pleasing so far as I am concerned in the sight of a regularly constructed section of honeycomb with every cell evenly capped with pure cream wax.

It is as wholesome as a farm cheese wrapped in its muslin wrapping, the way it comes from the loft or the cheese press. Once in a while someone would come to buy a section of our heather honey, but it was never advertised, being worth only a few pence in a day when the best farm butter might fetch less than a shilling a pound and eggs were sold for far less than a penny each. There was one occasion when someone came for. honey when we had none to hand. It was almost spring. The bees were living on their stores and the weather was cold. Fresh honey from the hive had been prescribed for someone who was at death's door. Grandfather looked at his beehives and sighed. He, too, had great faith in honey, but the hive he touched in this cold weather would almost certainly perish and he wasn't sure that much honey remained in any of the boxes. At last, with heavy heart, he went out and robbed his biggest colony in the cause of mercy. The thankful relative of the sick person hurried away with the honey which was given freely. He would come back, he said, and make sure about the colony that had been robbed. Accepting the honey was one thing but killing the hive was another. Grandfather wasn't mistaken. The colony died of a chill. He brushed them out and refurnished the hive ready for the first swarm that came, but the man who had had the comb that cold spring day didn't return. Perhaps he was too stricken with grief at the death of his loved one - or too jubilant at her recovery to remember the bees and their owner. Troublesome as the bees were to those who considered they had more important things to do, everyone was saddened at the death of this colony. Never again would such a brutal course be resorted to, though the King himself asked for honey to ease his cough!

Year after year we went through the ritual of beekeeping and management. Year after year in the early summer we took panic at the swarming time and, it seemed, year after year Grandfather built new hives and renovated old ones. He knew very little about the things that are today common knowledge among apiarists, though he searched for the queen and did his best to control the swarming and safely hive new colonies in quarters specially prepared for them. Sometimes the work of turning hay to get it dry before the onset of more rain prevented him from doing all he might have done and a new hive was set up in an upturned margarine box laid on a wooden kitchen chair, to be rehoused later on. Sometimes he wasn't blessed with the right weather on the right days and more urgent farm work prevented him from gathering the honey harvest, but he was an incurable bee-fancier and like the best of them, he was immune from the effects of bee-stings. Not for him the blue bag or the fomentation. He would feel round his collar and discover a bee working its way down to his chest and the wandering bee would be gently lifted out and placed on the window ledge so that when it recovered it could slip out under the open window and fly straight back to the hive. There was a certain vanity in Grandfather's identification of the bee he found on his jacket or among the hairs of his beard and when he released it he seemed to see it flying all the way back to the hive in which he knew it belonged.

Old country people have many superstitions that concern bees. It was probably simple neglect that caused all those bees to die that spring when the old man died. It may have been they were short of candy, or felt a colder winter's blast than usual, but when Grandfather went to his long home his bees went too. Perhaps it was a similar coincidence that befell us when my father died. He died in the early spring of the year and his fourteen colonies of bees didn't come through that spring. They hadn't been deprived of any of their store in the previous summer, when my father was too ill to attend to them himself and I was too timid to take arms against them, even with all the tools of the trade close at hand.

7

Bringing in Harvest

Unless you have lived to watch the corn grow and ripen, and have known that peculiar excitement that comes to a climax in autumn, it may be hard to understand what harvest meant in the days before the combine and the baler. Harvesting now is a great deal more quickly done and everything is virtually cut and dried and tidied away in a matter of days from the time the corn is ripe. Stubbles are left long and a field of tight bales pleases the cubist more than the landscape artist, but for all that the corn must ripen. It may stand tall and green and sappy for seemingly endless weeks if the sun is continually obscured by passing clouds. July is generally a wet month everywhere, but it is wetter still, and more overcast, in the north, I think, and however well equipped the farmer is, the religious superstition of the old peasant still sees something fitting in his waiting for the sun to ripen the corn. Man is not God. When I was a small boy if people didn't get down on their knees and pray for a good harvest, for the rain to hold off and the crop to be brought safely in, it was because they worked hard and work was a prayer in itself. When all was done they gave thanks, but God helps those who help themselves, and they all helped themselves, even if it was still a wicked thing to put horses in a binder on a Sunday.

I used to get under their feet when the time came to haul the binder out of the black shed where it had sat brooding for ten months of the year. Getting the binder out meant that we were almost on the brink of the greatest effort of the year, a more protracted effort than the steam-mill threshing-day, as urgent as hay-making, but a far, far bigger task. The binder's joints were likely to be stiff and creaky. It had been a perching-place for the more venturesome fowls. It was bogged down in the litter on the floor, the residue of peats stacked in the big tarred shed, the litter of straw and hurriedly stored hay. It trundled out into the court, a squealing, rattling monster with its working parts in need of cleaning because of those roosting chickens, its stored-away sheets needing darning or patching, its cogs greasing, its chains turning and its levers, for lowering the knife bar, checking over. It often seemed that it would never be itself again and would never perform its urgent task, rock and sway and hurry round the rapidly diminishing field, with its great wheel getting polished and shining, rolling over miles of stubbles and countless boulders.

Grandfather was the binder doctor. He knew it as a doctor knows the functional parts of the body. He listened to it and studied its weaker organs, used keys and hammers, and sometimes the fire, to mend or tighten parts that were the worse for wear. He put the sheets on the roller and tested the knotter, was liberal with the oilcan and sharpened up two or three sets of knives.

In the fields the corn was ripening from a pale green to a pale gold - acres of oats and barley and sometimes rye. Oats, however, were the important crop. We had more oats than anything else, oat-straw to bed the standing-in cows in winter, and to make the horses comfortable in the stable, grain to be bruised and fed to the stock in mash, taken to the mill and made into oatmeal for our porridge, or exchanged for white flour. The whole economy depended on the milking-cow, and the cow depended on the corn. The gathering in of the corn was a challenge that every member of the family had to face. We were all harvesters. While no one knew the date on which harvest would begin, for corn ripened the way the first swallow came on the ridge of the barn or the geese came south in October, there were certain arrangements that had to be made in preparation for that day. We had to be sure that we had all the help we could muster. We had to 'wage' harvesters and everyone else in the countryside was concerned to do the same. We could get an odd man here or there who would promise 'a day', but it was necessary to be more sure of help than any casual promise. Grandfather would 'write away' for harvesters. An agent across the water in Ireland would

Grandfather working in the fields of North Clutag

arrange contracts with small farmers prepared to come over and work in the cornfields of Galloway and other parts of south-west Scotland. It was an ancient custom, this hiring of harvesters, and one fraught with difficulties and dangers. Not every Irishman who came was of the same religion or worked well with his fellow-countrymen!

To ensure as little friction as possible it was necessary to warn the agent that if he engaged one Catholic harvester it would be wise to see that he was partnered by one of the same faith. They could go for a Saturday drink together and to church the following morning without breaking one another's heads, as they might if one were protestant and the other acknowledged Rome. It was seldom that the agent made a mistake but there were times when the bottom of the barrel had to be scraped. The adherents of King Billy and the supporters of the Pope couldn't always be isolated or insulated from each other. It wasn't hard to tell which was which, though it would have been difficult to define the precise characteristics that indicated that a man was of one faith and not of another. It didn't matter whether they went to mass or stayed abed on Sunday morning but it did matter when their religious differences affected their work and one whistled little snatches of King Billy to add fuel to the fire of their hatred. Grandfather was too tactful to intervene and did his best to make his harvest team work amicably together. No Papist lifted sheaves while a grim protestant let him struggle with the reaper bearing down upon him and the following year Grandfather would insist that he must have all of one faith, so that the harvest might not have this increased hazard. The harvesters were best when of one religion for then they put their backs into the work to get it done.

The contracted harvesters were sometimes men who had come before and the family knew them. They had little farms of their own in County Down and left their wives and families to bring in their own small harvests. They had a burning desire to get the work done so that they could return to their native place and it was only when there were breakdowns or periods of wet weather that their spirits fell. They were almost always a lighthearted, cheerful set of men, as hard-working as any of the men of Galloway. They would work late and continue by moonlight, if they were allowed to do so, but dew falls after dark and the canvas sheets of a binder quickly shrink and tear if too much moisture gets to them. The tilting-reaper was a different proposition, of course, and could be 'served' on a clear moonlight night, but it involved much more labour, lifting and tying sheaves, and was a slower way of cutting corn. Sometimes when the contracted harvesters were flushed with excitement at the prospect of an early finish they would volunteer to work by the moon but the ordinary hired helpers would protest. They firmly believed that it befitted a man to perform his allotted task while it was still day! What recriminations and grumblings there would be if, after a proposal to work on had been rejected, it rained the following morning!

Rain produced frustration but lying corn was an annual bugbear. When this happened the corn had to be lifted with a rake handle and set against the knives of the machine so that it could be cut without waste or the machine bogging down. Worst of all, however, was the crisis that came when the binder broke down and some vital part was found to have fractured or worn away. This kind of crisis could come at any time but it hardly ever occurred when the last half acre was being cut. Nor did it happen early on, but nearly always in the middle of the task, on a clear bright day when everything was going well, when the horses were thudding along, the tall corn was rippling over the knives and tumbling under the flail and everyone was in high spirits, the bird singing in the tree and the sun blazing down upon us. Such a sudden coming to a halt was unreal. The silence itself was unnatural. It was never long before everyone was out of the rhythm of the work and most of the harvesters were sitting on fallen sheaves, searching their shirts for seeds that tickled their skin, or drawing on stumps of cigarettes hastily put into the pockets at the onset of the afternoon's labour.

While the horses dipped their heads to snatch mouthfuls of

growing corn, tearing it up by the roots, Grandfather would be on his hands and knees studying the machine to see what had caused it to come to a standstill. It didn't take him long to find the cause but it sometimes took a while to decide on the best course of action. He would pull out his watch and look about him. He knew who had an old binder of the same model and mark. He wondered if it had a spare part on it, and how long it would take to replace the broken piece. He decided whether the horses would be taken away, fed and watered and put out to graze, yoked to the reaper, or kept in the field while the spare part was obtained. No neighbour who could oblige in such circumstances would dream of refusing help. Sometimes the broken part could be mended at the smithy and Grandfather would hurry off down there to make a repair so that no more than an hour or two would be lost. Sometimes the reaper was the only way unless another binder could be borrowed. The harvesters were impatient to get on. They knew a harvest day to be the precious thing it was, a God-sent day when it was a man's duty to toil and reap the field as quickly as he could.

Once in a long time the trouble would be serious, so serious that a neighbour who had suffered no setbacks would send all his men to help out and perhaps bring implements too. Harvest was a war in which the whole countryside was engaged and sympathy produced help wherever a man was in difficulties.

Not every year was harvest over in a month, or even two. Sometimes it dragged on for three, because rain came, because the corn went down more than in previous years and couldn't be cut with a binder at all. Sometimes even the old tilting-reaper proved useless and only mowers could clear the great areas of broken straw and tangled ears. Between whiles, when it rained, work of some sort had to be found for those who had nothing to do. The harvesters hired for the contract expected to work at those things connected with harvest. They kicked their heels on the corn chest in the stable, sat smoking in the barn, laughed and told tales and sometimes quarrelled until they were persuaded to roll grass ropes, ropes made of light fibre and not capable of taking any strain, but ideal for holding down the thatch of a rick. Rick-thatching was the very last operation at harvest but it couldn't go on unless the ropes were already rolled and sorted. Expert rope-rollers would take a pride in rolling neat little coils of rope the thatchers used when going round and round a rick, constructing a sort of network of rope to keep the thatch firm. Hanging from the network of rope would be one or two draining tiles or old curling-stones to keep everything secure in the worst of winter's gales. The harvesters, according to their willingness, coiled neat bundles of rope or made a careless job of the thing, but they did it to overcome boredom and frustration while rain dripped from the slates of the steading and wet, bedraggled fowls crowded in the doorways of stable, cartshed and turnip house. If one of the harvesters had a mouth-organ or a melodeon he played while the rest worked, and songs were sung, some of them old, sentimental songs, ballads never yet set down but learned by word of mouth.

To this I was a spectator. I would carry tea to the men in the granary or the stable and listen to their ribald jokes but when they were in the field I had to be kept out of the way. Many a farm child had met with an accident in the cornfield. Grandfather solved this problem in a practical fashion by fitting another seat on the binder. I sailed round with him while the corn was cut, well out of the way of the great feet of the Clydesdales or the running knives that brought the corn to the canvas. I never was afraid of horses after that, except perhaps, ponies. I loved the draught horse, the magnificent beast that thrust his great shoulders into the collar and struck the soft earth with his hindfeet as he pounded uphill, making the binder shake and vibrate, disgorging a sheaf every few seconds.

The sweat and toil of harvest is something I can never forget. It seems strange to me to see the way the tractor draws the binder at such an even, unhurried pace, the way a combine crawls along leaving its trail of bales and tied-up bags of grain. Can this be harvest? I ask myself. Are all the men who were men when I was a boy, dead and gone now? Where are the horses, the

Bringing in the harvest—Grandfather taking liquid refreshment

beasts bred to work alongside man, from the day he ceased to be a hunter and began properly to till the soil? I shall never ride upon a horse-binder again, or drive one, as later on I did, cutting acres of corn, a harvester in my own right.

Nothing lasts for ever, even harvest in the north as it was in those highly unmechanical days. The rake would soon become the only implement left working in the field. The last cart would go jolting and swaying to the rickyard, bouncing over the boulders in the road and coming to its final mooring alongside the last, almost completed rick. The harvesters would make their harvest dollies or plaits from the last straws, and laugh and talk and take a dram with the old man, perhaps. They forgot the grey days when the rain drifted in from the sea and they had struggled to cover the binder with a tarpaulin to keep the sheets dry and then ran to shelter under a dripping rowan tree. It was all over, the ploughing, the sowing, the reaping and the mowing. They were going home. Laugh when a thing is done because it is good to look back and remember that you could laugh!

Early in the morning, before milking-time, the Irishmen would be ready for the road, waiting with their clothes in a bundle tied with bindertwine. We took them to the boat train and perhaps they never sat at our table again. They had taken their wages. They had shared our labour and our heartbreaks. It was all done with. Mick and Billy said their goodbyes. The pony whirled them away. They waved as they went and looked back at the neat row of ricks in the rickyard, corn all stacked and made safe for the threshing that would come in due time. It happened once every year, and when it was over we took breath and waited a few days before going out to set about the same task to be done before the same cycle began again.

Potato-picking was never called harvest. It never had the same urgency, the same feeling of struggling against the relentless change in the season from summer to autumn with its rot and decay. Everyone, or almost everyone, took part in gathering in potatoes. We were over the hump of the year by then and it hardly ever rained, though there might be a touch of frost in the air. A mellow sun and a cool breeze would quickly dry the skins of the potatoes and they looked good on the rich black earth in which they had grown, but a potato field in autumn is a sad sight compared with the same field in summer. In summer it has a certain beauty of its own, an evenness, a rich green dotted with blossom, a scent that is strangely appetising if you have ever sat down to potatoes fresh from the earth with a glass of good buttermilk to wash them down. The digging was done with a horse-drawn machine that kept its balance by means of two landwheels. The spindle of these wheels imparted drive to the digging-wheel which tossed the potatoes out against a sacking screen along with weeds and fragments of dried, shrivelled haulms. On a good dry day the pickers could barely keep up with the machine, even when the driver took frequent rests. Sometimes he got down and gave them a hand, but it was never the exciting business that corn harvest was, even when a covey of partridges was put to flight or a hare rose and went helter-skelter across the broken furrows. Once, I remember, I was pressed into service to carry small cans to the sacks spaced along the field, a task I didn't like at all, but I escaped, as I always did from tedious tasks. I imitated the ostrich, put my body, or as much of it as I could squeeze, into a can and rolled away to the gate. It didn't shame me when everyone stood and roared with laughter. I took to my heels and ran for my life. Potato-picking wasn't a proper harvest. It was an anti-climax.

8

Feminine Influence

Early in my existence I became aware of the strong influence which the female exerts upon the male. My earliest frustrations most certainly resulted from the interference by women in the things I had set myself to do. Even my grandmother, whom I dearly loved and who taught me how to set a snare, had a way of guiding me from exploring the quaking midden or following the hurrying ducks on their way down to the waterhole. For some reason I was discouraged from washing my clothes in the burn, steered clear of the old Bubbly - the turkey cock that claimed right to sections of the steading where he sailed to and fro like a schooner in a bay and thereby inhibited me about turkey cocks for years! The women didn't like it when I went off on my own to count imaginary sheep on some clover hill far out of sight of the steading, or took the dog to explore rabbit holes before I was tall enough to be seen above the whin bushes. These were male occupations that put black, muddy stockings on my bare legs, saturated my clothing, got me lacerated by thorns, bruised and sometimes bloody. The antidote was a course of treatment called civilization. My mother, had she been at hand, would have demanded intensive civilization, but the women of my grandfather's household had to compromise. They did so by cleaning me up, combing my hair, screwing a flannel so far into my ears that sometimes there must have been a real danger that it would come out on the other side of my head. They searched me for hen lice, dog fleas and other parasites, deprived me of insects and small creatures I adopted as temporary pets, sat me up to the table, all bright and clean, and made me eat shortbread one bite at a time, which resulted in an impatience over the business of eating that has remained with me ever since.

The author (wearing the cap) and his brother Robert on the tilting reaper

Grandmother was firm. My aunts were inclined to be indulgent, for I was 'the wean', and a wean could be forgiven almost anything. A wean couldn't help himself. He loved to delve in mole hills and chase piglets, challenge broody hens and make life hell for the domestic cats. There was one way to apply correction and that was to send him down to have tea with Miss Dunbar whose civilizing influence and refinement were respected by all who knew her. A certain natural cunning saved me from the extreme effect of Miss Dunbar's corrective capacity. I admit that I took the dear old lady's sweet biscuits, looked at the silver-framed photogravures of her family, tolerated her great fat cats that had plush covered footstools to themselves, and gave all the right answers when questions were put to me. The dear old lady, a retired schoolmistress who had a cottage away down at our road end, believed until her dying day that I was a sort of minor saint. I never believed in kicking against the pricks, even when I was four or five years old.

Miss Dunbar had probably been crossed in love and chose this lonely corner of Galloway in which to live with her pampered cats. Her cottage was cluttered up with footstools, rocking chairs and old rickety furniture. China dogs grimaced from the mantelpiece at 'Tisles' and 'Whistles', the fat cats. Faded pictures of walrus-moustached men and straight-laced women adorned almost every inch of the walls. The old lady dressed in the fashion of the previous century, to which she really belonged. She wore a crocheted shawl on her shoulders when she went out at dusk to call in her cats. She was never without a bonnet when she walked abroad. On rare occasions she would be invited up to tea and she came like a ship on a voyage, slowly and steadily sailing up from the march gate, helped by a stick, for she was unused to rough ground, having trodden only the flagged courts and tiled halls of a private school for the greater part of her life.

Miss Dunbar was good for me, they said. I was always on my best behaviour when she was about. The truth was she had the same effect upon me as the minister. I was forced to be the very opposite of the wild creature I really was. I said very little, and that was a virtue in those days. Little boys were to be seen and not heard. I didn't mind this very much. What conversation could the whitehaired, grand-looking old duchess have had with me on the subject of moles, hedgehogs or the mating of cats? The hardest chairs I ever sat upon were those in Miss Dunbar's cottage and I never forgot the smell of paraffin! She cooked on one of those old-fashioned paraffin burners that had a wick like that of an oil-lamp. Paraffin fume pervaded everywhere in the cottage. Even the biscuits and the sweets with which I was rewarded at the end of my ordeal tasted of oil.

I was a saintly child most of the time, a credit to my family and obviously destined for a life in the church! How I so successfully created this impression I never knew. It certainly took patience and a great deal of 'Thank you, Miss Dunbar', 'Please, Miss Dunbar', and standing back to let the old lady go out in front of me, mainly because her door sometimes stuck and the handle was a little high for me to reach! I couldn't escape being tea-partied at Miss Dunbar's and rarely did I manage to dodge the visits she made to Grandmother and my aunts. If I shuddered at the thought of being imprisoned in the sitting-room or the parlour while Miss Dunbar paid a social call, my aunts and grandmother revelled in the occasion, brought out the cakestand, the silver teapot, their best china and loaded the plates less heavily and more delicately than they were accustomed to doing when more robust visitors were being entertained. Miss Dunbar's voyage up the rough road and through the puddles was achieved without too much mud getting on her thin patent-leather boots or on the hem of her heavy gown, and much of the fume of paraffin was blown away on the journey, but I never sat down to tea without wishing she hadn't so many mothballs in her pockets or in the bag that hung from her hand on a long silver chain.

The civilizing treatment would wear off quickly. Sometimes it lasted only minutes beyond the old lady's departure. Sometimes, suspecting that the attempted cure hadn't worked at all, I was commanded by Grandmother or one of my aunts to see the old lady back down the road. On these occasions my end of the conversation was always monosyllabic and vague. I was watching the cornflower butterfly, the red-arsed bee, the yellowhammer or the linnet on the whin, while the old lady talked of 'ladies and gentlemen' and the virtues of being able to play an instrument and sing. Perhaps when we had reached her cottage she would reward me with a peppermint which until it was well sucked had the flavour of camphor or paraffin, or she would invite me in to help myself to my favourite sort of biscuit. Once I was free I went off like a hare, back up the road and over through the whins to see if the linnet really was nesting there or if I could poke the whitterick out from the stone heap. She should have seen me then! She should have heard my wild cries as I scrambled after the rabbit that dodged me in the bushes and yelled for the dog to come out and help me in the hunt! No, it didn't last, but washed off just as readily as the peat washed from my leg. I should have turned out to be a noxious little monster had old Miss Dunbar succeeded in civilizing me, a sort of Uriah Heep of the biscuit barrel.

Less gentle altogether was the influence of old Aunt Ellen, Grandmother's sister. Mrs Orr, as she was fond of calling herself, was refined, proud and, I am sorry to say it, not beautiful, having far too stern a countenance to earn any greater compliment than that of being said to be dignified. Mrs Orr rode a bicycle. She was one of the outstanding lady cyclists of her day in that part of the country for she thought nothing of riding right across the shire to visit her sister, climbing endless hills and going unhurriedly down as many long slopes, the carrier of her machine loaded with her luggage and her dress held clear of the mudguards by a sort of clip thing called a dress protector. Like Miss Dunbar, she sailed rather than travelled in the ordinary way. Her pedalling was steady and never unladylike. She rode with determination and she had ridden so many thousands of miles that it was almost certainly the cumulative effect of physical effort that had set her mouth in a grim line. When Auntie was expected the womenfolk looked out for her with the same anxiety the men displayed watching for the mill's* appearance on the road the

*The 'mill' in Galloway is the threshing machine elsewhere. A steam mill was one driven and drawn by a steam engine; a walk mill was incorporated in a farm building and driven by a horse

day before threshing. Every five minutes someone would go to the window and report that Auntie hadn't yet put in an appearance at the march gate, but then she had probably gone round by such-and-such a place to visit so-and-so or stopped somewhere to have a puncture mended. There were no great hazards on the roads at that time, hardly any cars at all, and if Mrs Orr felt that the wind was too strong against her she could load her sit-up-and-beg machine on the train and save herself pedalling something like twenty-five or thirty miles from Port Logan down on the Mull of Galloway. I can't remember that I ever actually saw Aunt Ellen arrive. Unlike the visit of Miss Dunbar, Aunt Ellen's visit couldn't be timed to the minute and I couldn't be held around the kitchen for hours. I generally contrived to make myself scarce and stayed away for as long as I could, or at least until hunger overcame my dislike of being corrected and disciplined as Aunt Ellen felt every boy should be.

Grandfather did nothing to rescue me from my fate. He was too diplomatic to cross swords with his sister-in-law over minor matters. Sometimes he would want news from her of old acquaintances living at the other end of the shire and I would be able to sneak out and make myself hard to find, viewing the world from the granary, the barn or the top of a crumbling straw stack where laying-away hens had their nests or cats curled up to enjoy the summer sun. Most of Aunt Ellen's visits were made in the height of summer. A lady's companion, she often went abroad in the winter and renewed her contact with the family by making a tour on her bicycle when she returned home. Delighted though my aunts were to see her I sometimes think her overbearing presence and what might be called her class-consciousness were as much as most of the family could stand. Grandfather, I remember hearing it recounted, had once been persuaded to accompany Grandmother on a brief visit to his sister-inlaw's 'grace-and-favour' lodge on the estate where she was employed, if that is the right word for the now obsolete occupation of lady's companion. On Sunday he and Grandmother duly accompanied Aunt Ellen to church and when the great lady emerged from attending service Grandfather was taken aback to discover his sister-in-law in the very act of dropping a curtsey. He had a strong, reverberating voice.

'Dammit to hell woman, what are you doing down there?' he demanded.

Grandmother was shocked, ashamed. Aunt Ellen was affronted. I doubt whether she ever forgave him, not that that would have worried Grandfather very much! A man was a man for all that. He respected the law and the supreme ruler of the universe but he didn't bend his knee to mere mortals unless they put a pistol to his head. God save the king, he would say, and add, 'if he pleases', the old oath of the subjected.

A very different woman from Grandmother's sister was Maggie, my grandfather's own sister. He was fond of describing Maggie as the ugliest woman you ever saw: she was just like a man. This was more than an exaggeration and was never intended to be an insult to Maggie, whom Grandfather loved. There was no disputing the fact that Aunt Maggie was big and broad. She was dignified. She had a warm heart. Everyone loved her for she looked at the family with the warmth of kinship in her eye, acknowledging everyone as belonging to the clan and, by virtue of blood, as being excused weakness, poverty, or even meanness, which was not unknown in a hard farming community. Being my father's eldest son and the grandson of her brother, who was the head of the family as successor to Auld John, my great-grandfather, I was carefully inspected by Aunt Maggie every time we met. She showed her affection by pinching my cheeks. This always inflicted more pain than she knew, but I couldn't help loving her. I recognized the affection in her regard as she sat there like some ancient queen, the epitome of peasant strength.

When there was trouble in the family, a crisis of any sort, Maggie had to be informed. When someone closely related died and was about to be laid to rest they sent for her, and she came down out of the 'wilds' of Ayrshire wearing her mourning. She invariably engaged a 'hire' to bring her and when she arrived

Tammy at full trot with cousin Norman riding bareback.

everyone cried a little and had to be consoled a little, clasped to her breast. They might keen for a while and talk of those who had died in the years past, and then Maggie would examine whatever members of the younger generation were there to be shown off. Grandfather would help himself to a dram and talk to Maggie about farming and the fortunes of the family in hard times, after which she might walk out beside him to look at a horse or a cow and then come back in to take an enormous supper. She was a big woman and although she was sparely constructed and hadn't an ounce of fat upon her, she needed a fair helping of food to keep her going! Grandfather might monopolize her conversation for a good part of the time but invariably she managed to escape and talk with the women of the family about the things that particularly concerned them, the toil of the dairy, butter-making and cheesemaking, the value of working after pigs and hens, and finally, perhaps, the clothes they had bought when the sheep were sold, or would buy if things looked up.

Women never attended funerals. Maggie came because it was fitting that kith and kin met when there was a bereavement in the family. Her visit was a ritual of a sort. Sometimes she helped to prepare a tea or dinner for the returning mourners. More often she was only there to offer consolation and comfort. When the day was over her 'hire' appeared again and she climbed into it after embracing every member of the family and looking keenly into their faces, and away she went, back north, into the mist and shadows of the hills that separated her from the countryside in which she had been born and brought up. We didn't see her again until some new tragedy was upon the family and then someone would say, 'Better get a wire off to Maggie. She should be here.' She came until her brothers had all gone to their long rest but I never knew when she herself died. It seems to me now that something must have broken down in the structure of family relationship. Someone should have engaged a 'hire' and gone through the hills to pay their respects to Maggie, Grandfather's only sister who was 'as ugly as a man'.

My mother's influence could only be exerted upon me when she came to stay while my father had a holiday long enough to allow a visit. That she was generally dismayed to find me wild and unkempt I had no doubt. While she was with us I wore boots and stockings and was no longer allowed to run barefoot. My hair was combed at least ten times a day. I was washed oftener in a week than I had been in a month. I was discouraged during her stay from associating with the ploughman or the byreboy, and kept well out of earshot of the oaths that were sometimes used when a wayward cow went on the rampage and tore through corn or jumped the hedge and browsed in the kitchen garden. I wasn't mollycoddled. On the contrary, I was subjected to a severe discipline that resulted in my going to bed when the evening was still young and certainly before the kitchen filled up at supper time and the men exchanged rude comments and laughed ribald laughter about serving-girls and sex. Perhaps the thing that mother should have been most grateful for in this severance from her first-born child was the fact that she never needed to acquaint me with the purpose of sex. I had seen it all. I knew about it just as I knew that the yellow lilies would bloom in the old stackyard every spring. Once, curious to know what was going on when the groom arrived with a stallion at stud, I almost stood on my head to peer under a door. Grandfather found me there. 'Here, son,' he said gently, 'this isn't the way to look at a stallion serving a mare.' He took me by the hand and we stood watching the mating. I never thought of it afterwards as anything but a perfectly natural act common to all animals, men and women included, but I could never have told my mother this, and she might have found it hard to believe that I had acquired anything but a crude impression of an act that is only dirty or indecent to a dirty and indecent mind.

9

The Trotting-horse

Tammy was young and full of fire when I first knew him. He was the sleekest looking pony I ever saw, proud, highstepping, hard-mouthed and so fast that his hoofbeats were like a frantic drumming. His mane danced and streamed behind him. He was as graceful as a young deer. He was more than all that. He was the idol of the family and I suppose he knew it. If he went like the wind, and he did, uphill and down with the gig swaying dangerously and the grit flying from the wheels, it wasn't so much frightening as awe-inspiring. Tammy couldn't bear to be passed by anything else on four legs. He wouldn't allow it to happen, for he would trot to burst his heart first, his head coming in close upon his chest, his neck arched, his nostrils dilated and flecks of foam flying back from his mouth and falling on his flanks.

Grandfather's pride in the pony was matched by the pony's pride in himself. They were the most formidable combination on the road in a day when farmers loved to race one another, especially when they had taken a dram and had been bragging about the speed of their ponies. It wasn't easy to handle Tammy in his tantrums, when he reared and pawed the air and walked backwards instead of jogging along as more docile animals were wont to do. It wasn't easy to hold him when he brought his forefeet to the road and sprang into the collar, for then he trotted so fast that not only the spokes of the wheels vanished in a blur but his forefeet couldn't be seen either.

He was incapable of breaking the trot. He could neither gallop nor canter. He had the blood of fine trottinghorses in him and the fire that all fast horses need. Cry 'Whoa!' and your cry echoed in the woods, for he could not be held back by cries of alarm. Hold hard, haul upon his mouth with all your strength, and he tucked his head in in such a way that the leverage was nothing and he ran even faster than before, but talk to him, if you knew the way to talk and could cajole, soothe, persuade a highly strung creature to listen, and he might come to a slower pace and stand still. There was only one person who could work this miracle when Tammy was a young horse and that was his master. They knew one another. Somewhere along the road they had tested their wills upon each other in a wild contest that carried them past a rumbling threshing-machine crawling from one farm to another. They had rushed in and out of ditches and banks with the wheels throwing up mud and had come near to breaking necks and ruining slender knees. Grandfather had raged and stormed and Tammy had set his ears and they had fought it out time after time until they knew one another and loved one another like schoolboys who have exchanged blows until their strength has gone and hate turns to love.

Trains and steam mills worried Tammy, and the newfangled motor cars, when they began to trundle along the dusty country roads, going through long avenues of fir trees like prowling badgers or hedgehogs. People worried him too, when they came to admire his fine head and pat his neck. He had no time for mollycoddlers and petting women. He was a wild animal and he loved to run. On a still summer's night when Grandfather was away from home the family would listen for his return. The sound of the trotting-horse was unmistakable. It carried on the still air. When it was first heard Grandfather's progress, the exact location of the gig on its way along the public road, could be predicted. They were coming and coming like the wind, leaving barking dogs and wondering cottagers behind them, as near to flying as man and horse could be. It was like this when Grandfather headed for home when the market was over, but he contrived to hold Tammy back as well as he could so that some other returning farmer could come up and attempt to pass. A whispered word made Tammy run just a little faster, and a little faster yet, and a little faster . . . but who could stay with him? Who had such a pony? No one in the whole shire, in the whole of

Galloway perhaps!

Tammy became celebrated for his speed and the old man was known for his craftiness in encouraging rivals to take him on. Let them canter or gallop, they could make no better progress for a light gig rocks too much for any pace other than the trotting-horse's way. Coming back from market, the out-distanced challengers would be strung out over a mile or more and in the end Tammy and the flying gig would disappear from their sight. Sometimes Grandfather pulled in somewhere to take another dram and let them get ahead of him again, so that he could come up on them like an express train, feigning complete indifference to his pony's fast pace, smoking his pipe and giving a casual wave, but holding the reins firmly between his knuckles and gently pulling Tommy's head back to his chest so that he seemed to run as though there was nothing on earth that could stop him. 'That's the boy, Tammy. That's the boy!' the old man would say warmly, smiling in his beard. 'Go past them! Go past them all!' and Tammy's ears would flick back and forward just once or twice. He knew the game. He loved the race. The very devil was in him. They were of a kind, he and his master.

At first Tammy had frightened the family as much as he fascinated them, but gradually they tamed him after a fashion and he submitted to their petting just a little, tossing his head when he had had enough, showing the whites of his eyes when they annoyed him. He wasn't an ill-tempered pony but he wasn't a hack to be led by the poll and quietened with sugar. He would kick up his heels when let out to pasture and trot round and round so fast that when he stopped he would skid on all fours and snort once or twice before going off at a slightly slower pace, enjoying his freedom and independence. He was the most admired animal we ever had. It was no wonder that Grandfather had refused £100 for him before he was a year old. An ordinary pony could be had for something well under £20, but this was no ordinary pony. Tammy was a luxury, an indulgence, a sort of talisman. Everything the family did was a communal effort, a demonstration of loyalty and solidarity. It followed that we all believed that

Tammy was the fastest pony in the shire and would never be beaten. He was unique and everyone loved him. When farmers whose ponies hadn't done so well against Tammy in those wild road races looked for revenge they came to Grandfather and suggested that he might enter Tammy for a trotting-race on grass. Tammy wasn't by any means the only trotting-horse in the shire. Not all of the best trotters were on the road on market days. Wouldn't it be a good thing to see just how fast he was?

Grandfather couldn't resist the challenge. He looked about for someone who could ride a trotting-horse and not merely sit in the saddle while the horse ran. He found a man, a neat little man born to the saddle, a man who had ridden and broken hundreds of cavalry mounts, mustangs, trotting-horses. He was the perfect rider for the perfect horse. Tammy would never be beaten! Let them bring ponies from the other end of the shire and beyond!

The bargain was made. Tammy was saddled and ridden. He must have known what was expected of him. If he had gone like the wind in a gig he ran even faster with a rider on his back. The little man dismounted and said he had never ridden a better trotter.

It seemed a long day when Tammy was taken to show his paces because the races were at the tail end of a cattleshow programme. By the time the pens of sheep, the milking-cows, prize bulls, mares and foals, geldings and the rest had all been judged, the spectators had been more than once to the beer tents or the hotels up in the town. They were ready to shout and cheer and back their fancy. Some exchanged blows with equally truculent neighbours which did nothing to calm a highly strung pony held at the bridle. Small boys who had encroached upon the course had to be shepherded back to safety behind the sagging ropes, and bits of paper and other abandoned articles gathered from the field in case they frightened one of the competing animals. Used as he was to the peace and quietness of the remote farm, Tammy was difficult to contain and Grandfather was hard put to it to keep him back, especially when he forced his head into the crook of Grandfather's arm and tried to go.

'Hold still now, there's the boy,' Grandfather would say, over and over again.

When the boys had all found squatting-places or peepholes between the legs of their elders and the general clamour had died, the ponies would be released to trot a few paces up and down, their saddles creaking, their tails and manes streaming, and the crowd getting an opportunity to fancy this one or that one and make wagers among themselves. Would the fine dark horse from the high side of the shire, the pony that had won so often in so many places, leave Tammy far behind? We knew it couldn't be. All at once each one of us had the second sight that came down from old Nan the witch! Tammy would win, though every pony in the race left him standing at the starting-line, but they didn't. When the starter dropped his rag and they were off the crowd began to roar. Tammy was there and they saw that he was as fast on the soft turf as he was on the hard road, or nearly as fast, and soon he was out ahead of the fine dark pony and his nearest rivals, his lead increasing step by step. When he came round our eyes followed him and never turned to see how far ahead he was. It was all a dream we had been through before. Our hearts were lifted up, we were singing inside, pressing one another's hands, transported, radiant.

'There you are,' we said quietly, our hearts still beating fast. 'Will anybody dare claim that this isn't the fastest pony in the shire?'

No one did. Friends shook Grandfather by the hand, strangers pressed forward to admire Tammy's sleek red flanks and the fire that was in his eye. Rivals and enemies - there were always old feuds in that part of the world - muttered about it being all very well but Tammy had gone off before the rag had fallen, or his clever rider had cut in on the corner and slowed a pony that might have taken the lead. What about the bending-race, anyway? We knew about bending-races, a sort of mad gallop from one end of the field to the other and then an in-and-out course between posts. Tammy couldn't gallop. He wasn't an animal to be hauled up and jinked through posts. He was a trotting-horse and nothing else. Freaks could win novelty races, things like musical chairs played by mounted men. A triumph was a triumph and not to be diminished by a competition that had nothing to do with the pony's ability to run like the wind.

There was one great moment yet to come, the moment when Tammy, with the riding saddle exchanged for trap harness, emerged from the mews of the Galloway Arms and took us home through the cattleshow crowds, the dallying farmhands, the excited children, the people who knew us and were partisan. How proudly we all sat in the gig while the old man acknowledged the greetings of those who had seen or heard about the race. Tammy set his ears and showed off more than he had ever done. He was surely aware that he was the centre of admiration. When the children ran behind he must go faster than he had ever done before. Ahead of us there would be cries of alarm, 'Here comes that fast pony, watch out, clear the way!' and the fast pony came, making us all grip the gig handles until our knuckles were white and pray that the fast pony wouldn't miss his footing and fall or the gig turn over and throw us all into a ditch. There was nothing else in life to be compared with this. It frightened us and it delighted us at the same time. It was only when we were far on the road that Tammy was persuaded to slow down and go at a more reasonable pace and then we would pass a homing cottager with a calm indifference, acknowledging his wave, but never saying that had he waited at the show he would have witnessed a race the like of which he had never seen. Tomorrow he would hear about it and remark with a shake of his head that we had seemed extraordinarily steady, as though we beat the best trottinghorses in the shire every day of the week.

Beat the best, Tammy did, again and again. If he ever won by a neck we didn't choose to remember it. If he was ever beaten, and I would swear an oath that he never was, then the disaster was one of such traumatic impact that it was obliterated from our minds as soon as it took place. We lived on with our pride undiminished. Those who looked us in the eye hadn't the courage, the nerve, to say that we had been humbled and Tammy was anything less than the fastest trotting-horse in the world. I was a child, remember, sheltered from tragedy. Idols were never tumbled. They grew bigger and finer with the passing of time and when I saw Tammy run in his last race, for which they would only accept his entry with a heavy penalty, he was long past his prime, yet he ran like the wind as he had always done, and Grandfather stood and watched him with a smile on his face, his cheeks reddened by the dram he had taken, as pleased as he had been when Tammy won his first. How old was he then? Well on in his teens, I think, and a little more round in the belly than he might have been, but his feet punched the turf and his neck was as finely arched as ever. He knew he had to win. Between his first race and his last Tammy got used to the admiration of villagers, townsfolk, creamery workers and cottagers. He stood to be admired and he knew every word that was said about him. He never slumped in the shafts and hung his head in the manner of old, weary ponies. Every mile he ran he ran with the same zest, the same enthusiasm for trotting. I had been astride his back more than once but, being no horseman, he frightened me. We fought one another when I took the reins of the gig, as from time to time, in my teens, I did.

One wild excursion lives with me yet. It happened at the end of harvest, when, with the last rick roped and everything tidied away, a single harvester remained to make the journey back to Ireland. He had to be taken to the boat train and I was chosen to take him there in the gig. We sat up late, talking about harvest, about hares on the hill and partridges in the root field, and harvests that had gone far worse. The moon was still in the sky at daybreak when I went out to yoke Tammy in the gig. The harvester gobbled his breakfast and joined me, and my younger brother came along for the ride. The clock struck four-thirty. The train was due in less than half an hour.

Tammy started at a fast trot and in a little while he was making a pace that made me wonder if I could pull him in. When I tried I discovered that he had run away with me. He wasn't to be slowed, uphill or down. In the half light we struck an iron gate that had somehow swung past its post and partly blocked the road. The ring of iron against the hub of the wheel was frightening. The gate crashed back. Tammy couldn't gallop but he couldn't have gone faster. The harvester said a few prayers, crossed himself and promised God to change his way of life. Up in the hills the Irish boat train churned through rocky cuttings and roared out into the open countryside. Dawn was spilling on the flat fields and putting long shadows everywhere, but we had no time to study the glory of that September morning. We were hell bent and in the end only the white picket fence saved us from a broadside collision with the train. One or two bleary-eyed passengers from Euston looked out at us in amazement as the badly shaken harvester wobbled away with his bundle of clothes and climbed into a compartment without as much as a backward look or a wave. I turned Tammy round and set his face towards home and we went off again at a spanking pace although this time I knew that we would arrive without danger of a serious mishap.

Tammy the trotting-horse survived the old man, which was a blessing, I think. When the time came he was pensioned off, put out to grass. He had been promised that he would never be sold and he would be retired in peace and comfort, no matter what happened, and so he was. No Arab ever loved his horse more than Grandfather loved that pony. I am sure they talked to one another in private. Those who know a horse well will tell you that an intelligent one equals and sometimes excels in intelligence the average man. It is man's ego and ignorance that makes him imagine that he is of necessity the finest work of the Creator. There are better dogs and better horses than the general run of humanity!

10

Peats and Coal

The moor farms were places where black-faced sheep and bullocks were kept and little else thrived save the moor birds, rabbits and adders. The farms were walled in by drystone, grey-lichened walls that ran away back, it seemed to me, to the far end of the world, crawling up long rocky slopes and disappearing into hidden hollows of round rushes, bog cotton, meadowsweet, stands of reeds with waterholes where fowl swam. Even as a toddler I had been taken for walks across these places, carried over peat drains and peat cuttings, rescued from heather almost up to my chin and warned about the sleeping snake. Adders when they were killed with a stick went on writhing and twisting and showed their dirty yellow or grey undersides, almost the colour of the veins on the hands of an old man.

We rented a peat moss because it provided a cheap fuel, because peats burned with a grand heat and an aroma more soporific than woodsmoke. The moor itself had a special fragrance on a hot day or after rain. The air was something special. It was as pure as the water in the spring, refreshed and cleaned again and again by the hanging clouds, the mist from the sea, the warmth of the sun. I loved nothing better than to be loaded into a cart along with the peat-cutting tools and be transported away to the peat moss for the day. Looking back at it now, I see those days in a timeless setting. Things had been as they were then since the beginning. The sun marked the time of day, the hours weren't chimed. The bleating of sheep was lonely and sad at times, but when the wind carried cloud fast across the heavens it seemed as though a special radiance was engulfing certain places and then the sounds of the moor, although they hadn't changed at all, were as joyful as spring, as happy as the cry of the peewit along the riverside fields.

PEATS AND COAL

The cart didn't go to the moss to make a picnic. A man's wages were involved and the man cut peats, long sticks of black bog earth in which were imbedded the roots of heather, the compressed foliage of a long-mouldered forest. It was slow and heavy work and generally the cutting had pools of water which, as the fresh layer of peat was lifted out, flowed into the newly dug place, strong in colour like stout, like the water of the burn when it came down from the moor, brimming its banks after days of spate. The horse was tethered to a large rock near the old rickety gate that gave entrance to the moss. The cart was set with its shafts to the sky. The sun was always in the heavens, but every once in a while the man cutting peat would straighten his back and wipe sweat from his brow and consider whether it would rain or not, for a shower would come running down from the horizon, as fast as the cloud shadows, and he would have to leap out of the cutting and lumber along the miniature cliff to pick up his jacket before his shirt became wet through. Sometimes the shower hung there for a while and it was wiser to go back to the cart and lower the shafts and take shelter beneath it while the horse stood and let the rain run down his unprotected head, munching on a mouthful of fine wet grass. There were small distractions. A grouse would rise and go cackling up to a mound, disturbed by a stoat, or some other fierce hunter living on the moor, or a solitary figure would appear on the skyline, looking down at us, or perhaps only looking in our direction, trying to locate sheep or some straying bullock long missing from a particular place. Once in a while a cyclist would be seen on the grey road and the man cutting peats would stop and consider which of the moor families the cyclist belonged to, and who he or she might be, Dan or Tom, Mary or Lil So-and-so from up around the school, or the end of the loch, the long planting or the shepherd's cottage. No doubt the cyclist, too, enjoyed a similar sort of speculation about our identity, the man and the child, and even, perhaps, the name of the horse. For the road was long and lonely and crossing the moor everyone was out of time, beyond the bell and the ticking of the clocks.

85

There was nothing to show on our return home. Peat newly cut could only lie where it was laid until it dried out. Another visit would be made to set it up in little pyramids of three so that the wind could blow through them until they became almost as hard as wood. If they were all carefully and evenly cut they would stack well but if they were set up too soon they would dry with a curl in them and would never be any good for stacking. An untidy peat stack always resulted in a great crumbling and waste in which the hens scraped, reducing the debris to a fine dust that was useless for burning. Peat-cutting was undertaken with considerable care. The barrow was used to bring the load to more solid ground where a cart could be 'built' or loaded. An uneven building meant that peats would tumble off and fall into waterholes and be lost along the way. Wasted labour was the most criminal waste of all. A man who squandered his time was destroying himself.

Bringing home peat sometimes involved a relay of carts, a picnic on the moss and much more activity than was involved in cutting or setting up peats to air. The days were selected as the shore picnic days were decided when the 'carry' was high. It generally fell out that men and carts were available between the end of hay-making and the beginning of harvest and the very height of summer produced a drowsy atmosphere along the moor road. Here young rabbits gambolled and there a small bird fed a clamorous late brood along the top of a drystone wall. Everywhere the horizon shimmered and images were distorted by the heat radiating from the peat banks and those great tracts of motionless bracken in whose green depths thousands of rainflies brooded and the foul stinkhorn grew. It was the picnic excitement that delighted me rather than the chance of a ride along the uneven pathway from the carts to the place where the peat pyramids dotted the ground like miniature corn stooks. The peat barrow had no sides and only an end-board. The board was high so that as big a load as possible could be built against it. It took some ability to balance the barrow without the whole thing toppling, but on the way back it could trundle along at a great pace. If I tumbled off the worst that could happen was that I might get a ducking in a mossy pool or go head over heels through the heather. We lit a fire among stones by the wall, careful in case peat caught fire, for a peat bank can burn for months. I remember the tea that was brewed had a peaty flavour although I drank very little tea and much preferred the water from the spring. When all the peats had been barrowed in and the last cart was loaded a place might be found for me in the final building, for I was too small to walk all the way home. The cart was built high, but of course the load wasn't nearly as heavy as it would have been had it been stacked with sacks of corn. The horse took its time, the moor trailed on either side, the sheep bleated, the birds sang and as always I choked back tears that anything so perfect ever had to end. I loved the moss as I loved the far-off blue hills, the crouching, whitewashed farms, the lonely trees, the landmarks of a beautiful countryside.

The peat was stacked immediately, if that could be done, for it was better to build before it rained. All moorland farms had peatstacks close to their doors, some of them as much as fifteen feet in height and several yards long. Ours was an arable farm and the little bit of 'moss' it contained had long since been exploited but we had peat like the crofters and the shepherds, and the rent, I think, was only a few shillings a year paid to the owner of the moor.

While I was small an alarm about peatstack ghosts spread through the countryside. It seemed that on one of the lonely moor farms a ghost had emerged from the peat stack and knocked on the door and the windows. This happened night after night and the old couple who lived on the farm were thoroughly terrified. Soon the same ghost, or one just like it, began to knock on doors in other places. The peatstacks either housed the ghost or provided a suitable place round which he could disappear. As the terror continued people who would normally have left their doors unlocked became reluctant to open them after dark on any pretext whatsoever. Our peatstack would soon have its ghost, it was whispered.

Grandfather was angry at this suggestion. He would fix the first peatstack ghost that showed face round our door, he promised. They would get one or even both barrels of his gun and they wouldn't disappear round the peatstack without leaving a blood trail and having two or three pellets in their hides! As for me, I had never been afraid of the dark. When the wind rumbled in blocked-up and boarded chimneys, when it whined in keyholes and moaned in rainspouts, I knew that it was the same wind that set the tops of the elm trees threshing and swaying, the wind that carried ungleaned straw from the harvest field and hawthorn leaves from the hedge. But peatstack ghosts were a different matter. They were ten feet tall, and black as the shadows along the side of the peat. They loomed and retreated. They tried the door-handles in the small hours when even the collie dog was deep in sleep, and they crept about, looking for a way in so that they could creep upstairs and murder us all in our beds. Imagination is a large part of everyone's life. It colours the day, it darkens the night. It builds and it destroys and there are no physical terrors that are half so real as those that can be conjured in the mind of a child. It was too late to tell me that ghosts didn't exist. I had heard my elders talking about the terror on the moor farms, the knocking, the awful horror of the darkest night in the loneliest places in the world. I could lie and think about the peatstack ghost and my mind filled with horror, my voice shrank to a husky whisper, my mouth went dry. I was ready to die from fear.

The peatstack ghost wasn't black, however. It began as a black ghost but a day came when it was seen to be a white ghost, swathed, as most ghosts are, in a white garment of some kind. It made frightful sounds and people still locked their doors and clasped their hands but it seemed to have a little more substance than had at first been thought. At last the most seriously plagued farmer, an old man who had only his wife for company, opened his door an inch or two after the ghost had knocked a few times and did what Grandfather promised he would do. He fired a gun at the retreating ghost and the terror ended that night. It seemed that two pranksters had decided to have a little fun with the old people and the game had become too engrossing by far until the lead whined past their heels and perhaps a pellet or two broke their skin. The haunting, which had spread to more than one moorland farm, stopped abruptly. It was one thing to play the part of a disembodied spirit but it was another to be disembodied! In a short time I, too, began to forget the creeping terror that felt its way along the whitewashed wall and gently tapped on the door and window, then rose to a height of ten or twelve feet and walked in the shadow of the eaves, a black, faceless, awful thing that went back into the peatstack and slumbered there through the hours of daylight. I have often thought about ghosts in particular places, read stories of hauntings and strange happenings, but the only real ghost for me was that peatstack spirit. He can still come up out of the past like a genie emerging from a bottle.

The beauty of having an ample stock of peat was somewhat offset by the dust that results from peat fires. The house must have been permeated by it, for peat burns away completely and the fire subsides in a fine grey dust that rises and floats away on the slightest draught. Another serious drawback was that those who sat by a great peat fire quickly lost their wits and fell asleep as though drugged, partly, I think, due to the fragrance of peat itself and partly to the rapid consumption of oxygen in a room with the door shut. There was always this tendency to shut out the night, to close the door and draw the curtains and enjoy that snug feeling. Many times those due to rise at five o'clock for the milking stirred at three and wondered what they were doing in a prickly horsehair chair before a comfortless fireplace. There was certainly no need of a sleeping draught when someone piled the fire with peat and settled to a glass of brown sugar, hot water and whisky, but it was a very different thing in the small hours when a gale was tugging at the house, hail hammered the windows, and the outer and inner warmth had gone. I don't know how it came about but by the time I was in my teens there was no longer a peatstack. The magic and wonder of those visits to the moss had gone for good. If peats burned on the sittingroom or parlour fire it was because some moorland farmer sent down a sackful, certainly never enough to build a stack, but one or two to remind us that there was nothing quite like a peat fire.

Although the womenfolk insisted on using the iron girdle over a fire of sticks our peat fires were supplanted by coal. There was no particular magic in this except that coal had to be hauled by horse and cart from the station and a wagonload ordered at a time. I don't know how many cartloads there were in a wagon but several journeys had to be made. It was a much harder task to shovel and load coals than to build a cart with hard dry peats, but there was a certain adventure in it. I used to ride in the empty cart on its outward journey and run behind or in front on its return, exploring the hedges and banks for the nests of birds, chasing young rabbits, stalking frogs and getting my feet wet in waterholes. At the station there were exciting things to be seen, bullocks in transit in cattle trucks, red- and blue-painted ploughs, harrows, binders and reapers, neat ranks of fertiliser in sacks with names on their fat bellies and odd items waiting to be delivered to farms and farmers we knew. The men loading coal had no time to explore the yard. There was no time to spare and when the last great lump of black shining coal had been shovelled on to the top of the load it was only a minute or two before the horse was led away and the cart went rumbling home, sometimes leaving a piece of coal here and there to mark the way. If a large knob fell the carter would sometimes turn back and carry it to the cart once again but if it was left on the road some frugal cottager would surely stop and recover it for his own fire. Often when we passed a cothouse the children would come out and trail along behind hoping that some accident might befall us and they would be able to run home with coal. At the farm the cart would be backed up into a drystone-walled corner and the drawbolt pulled. When the horse was led forward the cart automatically tipped and the coal cascaded down with a noise like a miniature avalanche.

It was always good coal, it seems to me now, bright and shining as though it had been especially cleaned before it was sent to us.

It remained bright and shining even after rain but it burned with a black smoke that was far less pleasant than woodsmoke or peat reek. There were cinders to be carried and scattered in damp places. Neither wood ash nor the residue of the peat fire had ever created any sort of problem. Progress it was, you might say, but we had lost one of the marks of peasant existence. We were reliant upon the pale, hollow-eyed fellows who toiled hard to bring coal from the deeps of Lanarkshire. We didn't know them and they didn't know us. Could they have come and dug peat on the moss, I think a lot of them would gladly have done so. They earned little more than farm labourers and the air, the cool breeze across the heather banks, and the sunlight would have worked wonders for them. We shouldn't have had to break with tradition and begin to pollute the air with sulphurous fume.

It is hard to say when we changed just as it is hard to say when it was decided to install a donkey engine to drive the walk mill, or to leave the pump to rust, never again drinking water from a spring that had served the kitchen for generations. A man should think hard before he decides that some new, labour-saving device is entirely a boon, that it is easier to have his bread cut for him than to cut it himself. The day will come when he will be at the mercy of men whose faces he has never looked upon, enemies of self reliance and personal dignity!

11

The Milking-cow

Morning was never at seven. It began at five, whether the sky was dark or not, and the cows were either standing in the byre or waiting near the gate to be herded in for milking. The pattern of the beginning of the day never changed whatever befell the family. One couldn't be reared in such an atmosphere of hustle and bustle without knowing the milking-cow and understanding that those who tended it were its servants, its slaves or handmaidens, completely and utterly.

Everything that went with the business of dairying became part of my infant background and impressed itself upon me indelibly and forever. I know the milkingcow better than any other animal, though I have spent all my life using a pen to earn my living and never owned a cow. The smell of hot, fresh milk is a sickening animal smell, no less unpleasant to the nostrils of a fastidious individual than the reek of a byre midden. The cow is an extraordinarily unintelligent, cud-chewing beast with a habit of swishing its tail and lashing out with its hind legs that doesn't endear it to those who come in contact with it for the first time. It is also a complaisant creature, an uncomplaining, rather sad beast that lends itself to the schemes of man in a manner that is surely a blessing for those who live without the green meadows, strap-hang on underground trains or study form outside the bettingshop. Every cow has a name and everyone, dumb or obstinate though cows may be in the mass, has a certain character, a personality known best to the man or woman who takes from it its quota of milk, the product of the meadow.

There were milking-machines when I was a small child, human milking-machines who devoted an hour or more to milking a certain number of cows. The very best milker could sit resigned to milking twenty or thirty cows, if need be, milking fast, expertly, stripping to the last drop of milk with a skill that the layman could never appreciate, but there was always more to it than that. A cow doesn't milk as well for every attendant, whether he uses modern equipment or milks in the peasant fashion of thousands of years ago. Our milkers were an assorted lot. My aunts milked. My grandmother was an expert milker. The byreboy milked, and the ploughman too. At times someone from 'down the road' came to milk. It depended how many standing-in cows there were and how hard pressed the ploughman was when fields had yet to be rolled, harrowed and cultivated. When I was five years old I often awoke to the alarm clock's dancing on a chest or dressing-table in an adjoining attic bedroom, heard the dog's hollow-sounding bark and the sound of the hooves of cows on the road, sounds that were a somehow reassuring part of life, sounds that I would enjoy as much now as I did when a small child. No one thought there was anything sacred in the silence of the early morning. A churn-lid clattered and jangled as it rolled over the stones. The byre door was thrown back. The dog delighted in barking. The pump-handle squealed as someone drew fresh water, and far down in the mist-hung fields, the peewits took wing and called their spring call. Miles away the same sounds were filling the air in places lying in the shelter of round green hills and milkers were squatting on stools, their cheeks pressed to the great round, rumbling bellies of Ayrshire, Fresian or Galloway cows, while their deft hands sent milk spurting and ringing into their milking-pails.

What a world it was, a world of milk, butter, cheese, scalded cans, the trickling of coolers, clogs on spotless dairy floors, blue-striped aprons, scrubbed hands and little milking-caps. Morning was at five, but the milk wasn't always away - on its journey to the creamery - at the same hour every day. It wasn't always possible to get all the cows tethered, milked and out again at precisely the same time each morning. There were days when one wayward beast broke the boundary and wandered into the corn or found herself bogged in the farthest corner of the farthest field; days when some accident happened in the dairy, when the milk wasn't as cool as it needed to be before the churn lids were lifted on and banged down.

'We're late this morning,' someone would say, looking over to the east, listening to the train going through, or the sound of a neighbour's milk cart trundling along the public road while our own stood waiting by the opensided shed. 'Make haste!' they would say, and whoever it was would gulp his breakfast and take the cart away at last. The day wasn't rolling until the milk was away. Our shame was that at the creamery everyone would know that we were behind. There was always the danger that if this happened often enough the world would brand us as lazy, lie-abed people. If the morning was old at seven and we hadn't time enough, then it must begin at half past four! Who took the brunt of the frantic pressure? The womenfolk, the most expert milkers, those who could cope with the most awkward animals in the byre: the beast with tender quarters, the young cow given to putting her foot in the milking-pail, and the creature who could only be persuaded to yield her milk when a song was crooned to her. Grandfather would take out his watch and check it against one of the clocks and then go stumping out to find the cause for the delay. In the meantime those who were responsible for seeing that the milk was cooled and strained made haste slowly, slowly because a churn of milk that went sour through insufficient care was a great tragedy. The townsman was paying as much for a pint as the farmer was receiving for a gallon!

There were times when it might have been better to milk the cows to feed the pigs instead of carrying milk to the creamery and bringing back a set of rusty churns filled with sour milk. There was talk of a milk collection scheme, but as yet the local farmers were carting their milk to the creamery in light, spring carts or horse drays. On summer mornings there was excitement for a passenger on the milk cart. There was always a race to see which of two or three carts bowling along the road could get to the creamery first. Drivers would stand swaying on their feet on the front of their drays, imagining themselves to be Roman charioteers, perhaps, driving at a furious pace while the churns bounced and rattled and from each tight lid a little trickle of milk seeped and ran down, blue and watery looking.

When I didn't have to be wrapped up against a searing east wind that would chap hands and turn noses blue, I was often down in time to be taken on the milk run. Even when we encountered no rivals on the way the run was a delight so long as the sun was up. I loved every minute of it, the landmarks along the road, the blasted ash tree on the tip of which some mad, drunk tinker had hung a pony's shoe, the quarry where the stone-breaker sat on his inexhaustible gallery of boulders cracking them into a size suitable for road metalling, the cothouse where we were gravely saluted by the old shepherd, and the long hill that went down to the devil's elbow, a turn in the road blocked off to save two hundred yards, the new way running across a hollow.

'Here come the Barness boys,' the driver would whisper. 'We can't let them pass us now!' At once the reins would slash down on the horse's back and we would take off as though a tribe of wild Indians came in pursuit. The Barness boys would be convinced that their nonchalance no longer served any purpose and they had to let themselves go, uphill at full tilt, downhill without a hand going anywhere near the brake. Out in the quiet fields, someone abroad early to look his heifers over or attend to sheep, would hear the sudden clatter of the two milk carts and scratch his head and wonder if anyone thought what would happen if a wheel came off or one of the loads went over into the ditch and all the rich milk ran away. It never did, so far as I am aware, but that was more due to Providence than anything else. When the race began it continued all the way to the creamery bay. Only there did the driver relax and try to pretend that he hadn't really been urging his horse to a gallop. It was hard to deceive the creamery workers when the horse stood with its sides heaving, its nostrils dilated and gobs of foam hanging on its whiskers.

'You were well 'ahin this morning,' our man would say to his rival as he led the horse out to go home. 'I could hear you coming. Man you should stir yourself in the mornings!'

It was as well to set the spring cart going then so that the rattle of the wheels on the stony road covered the oaths this kind of remark provoked. Tomorrow we ourselves would have to look lively in order to be ahead. Whoever got in front weaved along the road and kept the lead. It was a point of honour never to be passed.

When we weren't bringing back sour milk for the pigs, which was a somewhat infrequent load, we had only to transport the empty churns we had taken in earlier. Back at home they waited to scald the churns with boiling water. There was always a cauldron, a set-pot, on the boil in the boiler house and a great fire of sticks kept it bubbling and steaming so that the churns could be sterilized. The most important duty of the day was complete when, on the way back, we met the postman and received from him the letters or bills that were addressed to us, and a newspaper a day old, posted from Glasgow. It didn't matter that what was new to us was already history to the world beyond. So long as days followed one another and the events were recorded, it didn't matter that we heard of the death of a politician when his successor was wearing his shoes. The newspaper wasn't opened or read on the way home. It was kept in its wrapper until Grandfather himself cut the string. He received it from the milk cart like a general receiving dispatches. He read it from cover to cover and shook his head or clicked his tongue at news of agricultural depression, falling prices for the farmer's produce, the increased cost of manures and seed.

'I declare to my God,' he would say, 'the Government cares nothing for us!' and what he said wasn't true. They cared less than nothing. A farthing a gallon on milk was an outrageous demand. What could there be in this business of grazing a cow and milking it - surely a game like sticking a potato in the ground and hauling it up in a few months' time to reap a tenfold reward? A cow gave milk as the rain fell from heaven. Politicians unfortunately knew nothing about the milking-cow or how milk came to their doorsteps in the morning. They didn't want to know. Weep and you weep alone. These red-handed, red-necked fellows were peasants - and a minority at that!

As a child much of the news of the day went over my head and past my ears without making any impression, which was not unnatural, but I wasn't insensitive to the reactions of the family. What brought despair to them was reflected in my world too. The cow was a sacred animal. Its birth and death both had a strong significance. I saw calves born, watched a sick cow die, saw a diseased animal burned in a great funeral pyre of logs, a secret, and for all I knew, illegal rite, the disclosure of which might have meant a condemned milk supply, a slaughtered herd, although this may have become enlarged and distorted in my mind with the passing of time.

Not all our work with cows brought only toil and despair. There were triumphs too. Once a year a special cow was entered for the milking competition at the cattle show. To enter for this event was a point of honour with the family. It required the careful tending and feeding of a selected animal whose milk yield would be measured and recorded for many weeks before the event. A cow had to be a good milker and a presentable animal as well. Competition was great. There were expert dairymen in the locality with fine milking-herds from which they could make their choice. Like preparing a horse for the show ring, the grooming of a cow was a job for a specialist. The family combination was formidable. It would have been an odd thing if an expert dairywoman like my grandmother, or either of her daughters, hadn't had exceptional skill in milking and feeding cows. It would have been odder still if now and then the cow they entered hadn't come somewhere in the prize money, but the prize of prizes was a silver tea-set for the champion milking-cow. Such a prize had a prestige value beyond compare. Win it once and you could sit back for a generation, recalled year after year when some new champion cow was led round the show ring. 'Remember when old so-and-so won?' the audience would murmur. 'He had a fine beast like this one,' or 'There never was a cow as good as that Ayrshire of old Willie Morrison's, the year it rained.' The year it rained, someone would hint, the milking-pail already had a pint or two of water in it before the competition began, but this was the sourness of a person who had never known the great triumph of winning the silver tea-set.

Our triumph came in a year when the sun shone upon us, when the turnips were clean and free from the red and white flowered weed, when there was no charlock, no milk thistles, no ragwort dotting the pasture, or so it seems to me now. Brocky, the cow that won the silver tea-set, was the most beautiful black-and-white cow that ever stood to be milked, and she was adorned with gently upturned horns, grey and blue in shade, fine, sensitive ears. She had a coat beyond compare, an udder that was large, and full in every quarter. I think my aunts got down on their knees and worshipped the beast. She became the personification of all dreams and ambitions. Prizes had been won before with lesser cows. The long boards above the stalls in the byre carried red-and-blue and green-and-yellow cards in abundance, more Seconds than Firsts, perhaps, but more Seconds and Thirds than Highly Commendeds, but Brocky was a champion cow. We knew it, we knew it, we knew it!

I sometimes think that the witch came back into the family at that time. Spells were cast to make Brocky win that silver tea-set and to confound all our rivals. Who can say, when a wish becomes a prayer? After much mollycoddling and endless attention to her daily needs, Brocky was led off to the farm below the town on the eve of the show. It was the custom for milking-cows to be brought within striking distance of the showfield in those days when transport wasn't readily available. Brocky was slowly and gently walked the four or five miles, haltered and kept clear of the verges where she might have got her flanks soiled. One of my aunts went to milk her that evening. This was important. Knowing how and when to milk a cow was part of the battle. Brocky was milked, watered and fed and left to herself for the night. In the morning she was watered and fed and taken to the showfield. The critical point was how much the disturbance, the road-walking, the different atmosphere, would affect her milk-yield. Needless to say, we were all there to see her next morning.

She was milked by the younger of my two aunts, the best milker in the family. The milk was carried away, tested for its butterfat, its quality and volume. There were many other cows being milked at the same time. The judging took an age. Time stood still. We no longer heard the bleating of sheep, the whinnying of horses, the hour tolled, the rooks in the trees, the jackdaws on the parapets of the jail, or the voices of the crowd around us. We were in a closed room of our own excited minds. We were willing Brocky to win. We were praying, conjuring up the witch, who was part of every one of us! There could have been no other result.

The 'broken-faced', black-and-white Brocky cow was the champion. She had won the coveted silver tea-set! All at once the world was full of natural sounds once again, children ran round squealing and laughing, and were scolded by irritable old men, the ground shook with the vibration of a proud horse's footfalls, the rooks were heard, the clock chimed. There was laughter among us and in the background. We knew, we had long known that it would be like this! Our pride was as much as we could manage. There were tears in our laughter. We laughed when we saw the tears and a sort of euphoria was upon us, as sweet and wonderful to a child as that wonderful Italian ice-cream over which they poured lime or raspberry flavouring. The family was drunk without having taken wine. There had never been a summer, or a cattle show like it, nor would there be again! The price of milk was threepence a gallon but who thought about that on such a day? In due course the silver tea-set was presented at the grand parade of prize-winners. In due course we went home. Whether Tammy raced that day or not I can't remember. The milking was late, I am sure, but we rode home breathing honeysuckle, meadowsweet, heather and the scent of old tea-roses. The sun never set on a more heavenly day.

12

Entertainments

Ours was generally a bustling, noisy household but sometimes it was quiet, for even the sooty-looking canary could not sing forever and there were times when a drowsy peace fell upon the place. There were times when the horizon was dark, when it seemed that the wet summer would last forever or a sick animal would inevitably die. By contrast there were times when a wild gaiety infected everyone, when the fret-fronted piano, that was tuned once in a blue moon, jangled out hymns and accompanied the singing of ballads, when one of the men played a melodeon and sang of the wild colonial boy or when he and Maggie had been young. Sometimes a violin was produced and people danced. The gramophone came on the scene. Orchestras played while toes tapped and I sat wide-eyed with the wonder of it all, for it wasn't one of those ear-trumpet gramophones but a little cupboard of a thing, the doors of which had to be opened so that the music could reach us. Music of a sort it was, but there were no critics of sound reproduction. The tenors were excused their tinny voices. What could we expect when they had come all the way from America or England, when the needle was as blunt as an elbow and the record already scratched because the dogs had had a battle and dislodged the gramophone while the great singer was doing his best?

Reels and strathspeys there were, military two-steps and new-fangled dances far less dignified than the waltz. All that was needed were enough people to make up a set and the room was cleared, the dogs and cats herded into corners or penned in the hearth, and a wild bedlam of national dances began to the music of the gramophone. It mattered not that those red-and-black tiles were scratched by hobnails, that dishes bounced and clattered on the shelves of the dressers and jugs of cream were overturned.

Ayrshires at North Clutag

The fire smoked, a curtain of fine ash rose to hide the sleeping canary, the oil lamp's flame was sucked up to the top of the glass where it glowed red like the last angry dawn and then sullenly smoked until the light in the room died and the fire threw grotesque shadows on walls and ceilings. 'Hooch!' the dancers would shout and again, at another ecstatic moment, 'Hooch!' and the dogs buried their heads in the curls of their tails and tried to sleep and pretend that the world hadn't gone mad. It didn't go on forever, of course. The gramophone had a habit of running down or the needle would stick. The enthusiasm of the dancers would be daunted and they would come to a dismayed standstill, looking like marionettes halted in the middle of a performance. But delays were never for long. 'Hooch!' they were away again. The cats shrank back. The dogs sighed. Once again the lamp puffed black paraffin smoke and dimmed as though it would go out for good. 'Hooch!' and they whirled with linked arms and almost lost balance.

Grandfather danced, despite his lame leg. My aunts danced, and the ploughman, the byreman, everyone and anyone whose joints weren't too stiff - everyone, except a small child, and for him the whole thing was a wonderful entertainment: the noise, the shrill sound of the gramophone with its awful tone, the clatter of feet, the laughter. When they danced, they danced. Nothing could stop them save exhaustion or the works of the gramophone going on strike. If this happened a crisis was at hand. Grandfather found his tools, pincers, screwdriver, hammer if necessary, and set about persuading His Master's Voice to emerge again. Invariably it did, sometimes after a pot of tea had been made, sometimes when the ginger wine had been tasted. The night outside might be peaceful and still or wild with the roaring of a gale. It made no difference. Within, a wild measure was being trod. Great Aunt Ellen forgot herself for a short time and was swung round in the reel. It was a miracle, with all, that shins were so little bruised and toes so little trodden upon. 'Hooch!', the wildest dancing in the world had produced no louder laughter, no redder cheeks, no greater delight.

It was all a great mystery to me, the beginning of this thing, the way it went on, the completeness of the transformation from peace to bedlam. The evening might be quiet with one reading under the spilled light of the oil lamp and another busy darning a sock and all that could be heard was the steady, melodious ticking of a clock and then suddenly the gramophone was out, the table pushed back and everyone was dancing. No one complained that it had been a hard day ploughing the old fallow or mowing in the five-acre. No one said anything about milking in the morning or the tasks that still had to be done before the light was turned out and everyone toddled off to bed. Dance, they said. All at once life had to be brightened, the house made to resound with the whirling of feet on tiles, the music of an old, scratched and sorely misused record. Dance, they said. Man wasn't put on earth to do nothing but toil. Sometimes he had to let himself go and do his best to remember the steps, whether he had once been correctly taught or not, whether he knew the refinement of the ballroom, had worn white gloves and ballroom shoes, or never danced in anything but farm boots in all his life. When it was over the house seemed to go abruptly to sleep, the rain spattered on the skylight, the wind moaned in the chimney, the last glow of the embers faded and the cats snored. Sometimes I sat up late and went to bed so excited, so stimulated by it all that I couldn't sleep even when I was enfolded in the softness of a chaff mattress. Everything in life is best understood by contrast, silence and song, tears and laughter, hunger and a full belly, the taste of wine and vinegar. In a strange way dancing was like wine. It put a light in the eyes of my elders, a glow on their faces. It transported them in happiness, even Grandfather who now seems to have been the most unlikely dancer of them all. In the morning my aunts repaired the damage, tidied the kitchen, dusted away the ash drift, set things back in their proper places and looked smilingly at the old cracked records. The gramophone went back into the cupboard down the passage until once again the mood came upon them and they danced.

There were other entertainments less hilarious, less abandoned, if abandoned is the right word. The mildest of them was surely teacup reading, a business embarked upon with a solemnity that might have pleased an ancestor, old Nan the witch. Not everyone could read teacups or was acknowledged to be good at the art, for that would have reduced the whole thing to frivolity and nonsense. Who would believe in the tall dark man who was to be encountered in 'a two' or 'a three' the numbers indicating a period of two days, two weeks, two months or two years, if anyone and everyone could make such pronouncements? Only a very select few had the way of reading cups. It was a woman's business, of course or almost so. Angus, a great friend of the family, was outstanding and no woman could equal his gift, but in the main, whether the reader was male or female, the reading was given to women. The tea was solemnly swallowed, the dregs of the cup solemnly swilled and the small quantity of liquid poured into a slop bowl. 'Ah,' said the reader after looking his audience over, 'I see a journey here in a two. You are to meet a tall man. He is not married and he has a lot of money. . . .' Almost at once there would be speculation about all the tall, comfortably-off men in the neighbourhood and places to which anyone might make a journey in two days or two weeks - or two hundred years!

'You may smile,' the reader of the cups would say reprovingly, 'but what I see, I see, and you can't deny me. I see it all here!' What could be said to prove things otherwise? Tomorrow had yet to come and there were things in the tea-leaves that even I could see, black birds, picks and shovels and trains, ships and shoes and hills and trees, black sheep and gravestones, signs of death. I must have almost frightened myself out of my wits at times, listening to the story of the teacup. Perhaps they gave me nightmares but Grandfather would call a halt and say that it was time I went to bed and time the women had done with their nonsense about symbols of death and bad news, coffins and black-edged envelopes being brought by the postman in two days, two weeks. . . .

'Have done!' he would command. 'Drink up your tea and put this rubbish out of your heads. Nobody is going on a journey.

Nobody is going to die. Somebody is going to be late out of bed and the milk cart will be kept waiting if this goes on. I don't need to read the cups to tell you that.' The teacups would be left on the tray and the reading brought to an end. Perhaps when they were washing up before going to bed my aunts looked reflectively into their teacups and wondered if they were to marry or remain spinsters, if they really were going on a long journey with great joy at the end of it. Perhaps they sighed as they swilled their fortune away and the tall dark man floated in the bowl, no longer a man but a tea-leaf..

There were other forms of fortune telling but none of them had the same fascination. Reading palms wasn't half so exciting and cards didn't stimulate the imagination the way a mess of tea-leaves could. Cards were for playing whist and whist was a serious business in its own right, a game for the long dark winter evenings when the blinds were down and the curtains drawn. The family were great card players and when the table was cleared and the cards were dealt there was very little small talk, very little thought about anything except what was trumps and who laid what cards. Again I was a spectator, studying the tight-lipped way Great Aunt Ellen played her hand, the way Grandfather hid all his cards in one enormous palm, the way the players watched one another, the look of triumph or dismay that followed the playing of a king or ace, even when I knew nothing of the rules of the game. There was very little laughter and long silences between the dealing of one hand and the next. 'Dammit,' Grandfather might say, 'I might have known she had the queen!' but that was all. Carefully he would mark his tricks on the back of an envelope, keeping a tally of his and his partner's triumphs. Sometimes, I suspect now, he cheated a little to annoy his sister-in-law. Sometimes he couldn't resist gloating when he won and Great Aunt Ellen was so obviously put out by her defeat. 'Ah,' he would say, 'it is no use playing cards unless you can stand to lose. If you can't take a whacking you shouldn't play!' and Great Aunt Ellen would mutter her disgust and throw her cards on the table and talk about the niceties of rules that suddenly became significant and would have been expedient to change defeat into victory had she thought of, and insisted upon, them earlier in the game. 'Well, we'll have done then,' Grandfather would say, smiling into his beard. 'I can't stand playing with women that take the huff.' Rarely did they have done, however. Downcast Great Aunt Ellen might be, but she was a determined woman and loved to take her revenge. She never gloated when things fell out to give her victory but there was a look of grim satisfaction on her face that she could never disguise. She was a firm believer in justice for others.

Somewhere between cards and teacups were those ballad-singing evenings that seemed to develop as soon as we had a visitor who had but the slightest reputation as a singer. All at once everyone short of Grandfather and Grandmother would find themselves standing at the piano delivering his party piece, snatches of some old favourite, the songs of long ago, love songs, sad songs. Poor Kathleen was taken to her home again though the colonial boy Tom Bowling had left his, was in his watery grave, and we listened to a song about grannie's highland home, a place so sad and forlorn that I could never understand why anyone wanted to see it again. Cousins sang, uncles and relatives of all kinds, strangers too. The moths were disturbed from the piano's fabric, the loud pedal squeaked, the soft pedal rusted, and no one seemed to notice if some of the keys were sticking and no chord was ever complete. One sang and another sang, and we all sang together, quite without self consciousness or inhibition. It was a firm belief that everyone could sing, everyone had a note of music in him somewhere, and a sympathy made the tone-deaf singer almost bearable to those within earshot. My father sang and I am inclined to think that he really was tone deaf, but he sang to himself and for himself to express an inner happiness, which is a good reason for singing. I was persuaded to sing when I was old enough to master a natural shyness. I sang 'Tom Bowling'. The darling of the crew died and brought a lump to my throat. It always puzzled me that he was supposed to have gone aloft after doing his duty below for sailors were buried at sea by being wrapped in a sheet with a weight tied at their toes before they were slid overboard.

Mary with the prize cow

Singing on Sunday was hymn-singing. No cards were played. It wasn't even proper to whistle, but there was a certain entertainment on summer Sunday evenings when various members of the household took themselves off to the 'preaching'. The preaching was at the schoolhouse down beyond the smithy. It was a much less formal business than going to the kirk, of course. It involved a walk along the honeysuckle hedges and the footpath leading on to the public road, and down the hollow between the drystone walls of fields on either side, here and there catching up with some neighbour also on his or her way to the meeting.

All the summer Sunday evenings had magic, with dogs barking far away, and cows lowing in the green meadows, smoke rising from cottages that had their windows heavily curtained so that they seemed to sleep in the setting sun. What the preacher had to say went over my head. I heard the rooks in the trees behind the smithy, the babble of the stream tumbling over the stones, the clip-clop of a pony passing on the road outside. I lived in a world of my own, unconscious of the hardness of the schoolroom forms and the smell of varnish but watching the bee on the window pane buzzing to be free. When we emerged again I walked in a dream, paying no heed to my elders, to the squeak of Sunday boots or shoes and the reverential talk of the sermon and the preacher's eloquence. I studied the black snail on the roadside, the cat running on the top of the drystone wall, the way the smith's bantams roosted in the garden bushes and how the smithy brooded on the Sabbath with a sort of sickness, a lack of activity, that was as unreal as death. It was an entertainment, an event in the week. It set in my mind a timeless picture of the past, the peace of a Sunday evening, the ticking of big, white-faced clocks with slow-swinging pendulums and muffled chimes, a sleeping world, to which I would belong forever, to which I can escape now when more than half my life is well behind me, and those who walked to the preaching holding my hand have lived their time.

We came back to the steading and generally had supper without the lamp having to be lit, which was somehow the way those summer Sunday evenings always had to end. Entertainment? Life itself was entertainment. It was never boring. It was sweet, like the taste of honey, rich like the fullness of blackberry wine, long matured in the crock, savoury like the flavour of oatcakes and strong cheese, and simple and fitting, like the bubbling of the porridge pot set to one side of the fire in readiness for tomorrow morning's bowl of porridge and cream.

'Who did you see at the preaching?' those who stayed at home would ask. Those who had taken note would say whom they had seen and who was absent, who was sick and who was away visiting a relative. If a neighbour had trouble with straying sheep, or lacked some special thing, that information was imparted to the family. It all provided a pattern to the background of our lives, small talk, a laugh, a sigh of sympathy. Sunday evening closed in on the family like an enveloping blanket, as the shadows crept across the court. The lamp was never lit while a streak of red or orange remained in the sky, the northern lights perhaps, the last glow of a perfect day, a day apart from the other days of the week. The ploughman or the byreman came back from his visit to his relatives, trundling his battered old bicycle into the side of the gighouse, the collie dogs stretched their legs and came to lie down beneath the kitchen table. The door was locked and the house at last went soundly to sleep.

13

Labourers in the Fields

The first heroes in my young life were ploughmen and byremen, strong fellows who were apparently fearless, simple men who sat and talked in the stable, talked about the ways of birds in the woods and the animals of the fields. They talked of other things, of course, things that I quickly came to understand to be the simple facts of life, the ways of servant-girls and their willingness or otherwise to be persuaded to climb drystone walls and roll in the sweet-smelling grass, their facility to produce unwanted 'weans' and ask for impossible sums of money to maintain the little strangers! Ten shillings was an impossible sum, a fearful price to pay for an hour in the hay, for a man might earn no more than ten shillings a week and his keep. A byreman 'waged' for ten shillings. A ploughman was worth a pound, especially if he milked as well. Good men were hard to find and lazy fellows it seemed were more numerous than crows. Many good men left the countryside to try their hand at farming in Canada and some, perhaps, took to their heels when their work in the hayfield bore fruit.

In the main our men were respectable, some of them the sons of farmers themselves, and not a few of them morally upright and much less hypocritical in their conduct than the elders of the kirk. There was John who carried me after dinner astride his neck all the way to the stable, a ritual that was only broken when there happened to be a downpour of rain. I worshipped John. No one displayed more bravery than he did when a great Clydesdale came rushing up past the midden hauling a cart of corn and threatening to slip and overturn the lot and perhaps crush John between the cartwheel and the wall of the byre. He could hold restive horses, sitting back on his heels with his legs braced, and he did it all without cursing the way some ploughmen did. He talked to horses the way they should be talked to, and there was never a moment when his heroic image was tarnished in my sight. John True was his proper name, or perhaps this is my romantic recollection of him, the tallest, straightest, kindest of all the men who worked for Grandfather.

John was followed by Jeck, and Jeck had his own special halo or glamour. He was an incurable poacher, a man who loved to go out with the gun. If he wasn't stalking the woods to bag a cock pheasant he was snaring the bog fields, catching hares and rabbits, or trapping something that was running the same path too often to escape his eye. They weren't as content with my worship of Jeck and the tools of his trade as they had been when John True was my idol, for it was plain that I could more easily learn the less useful virtues than the truly laudable ones. It was reasonable enough that I should be able to snare my dinner, but would it stop there, and having hunted the rabbit, what was to stop me following the old poacher into the woods and deciding that this was the life, the life without care or any regard for law? My grandmother taught me to snare but to be truthful she didn't give me any more than the rudiments. It was Jeck who taught me all the signs that indicate where a snare should be set. It was Jeck who influenced me, took me along the ferny banks, pointed out the place where the hare jumped to go over and slid back again, the place where the cock pheasant sat and preened himself and then slid under the fence wire to lose himself in the kale or the potatoes. I saw the stoat and the weasel while in his company, the water rat and the owl sitting asleep close to the trunk of the fir tree, the old tawny owl and the long-eared owl that haunted the planting. Jeck moved on. I was left to my own resources but I knew enough to catch a rabbit or a bird, and what I didn't know I gleaned from the peg-legged mole-catcher, whose amorous activity put most of the local rakes to shame, disabled though he may have been.

The ploughmen and byremen lived in the room above the kitchen, access to which was by the shaky wooden deal ladder and the

111

hatch leading to their bedroom. 'Up the men's stair' a number of things were stored in a sort of lumber corner behind the cupboard where they kept their clothes. Sometimes I was allowed to go up there and play, provided I promised to keep well away from the hatch. Balancing on a rickety table, and craning my neck, I could see through the skylight windows all the way in one direction to the march gate and, in the distance, the smithy and the schoolhouse, but the days when I went up to play with the lumber and peer from the skylights were generally wet ones. It was usually possible to see only as far as the march gate for generally a haze of rain obscured the landscape or a downpour distorted everything, even the outlines of the pine trees in the garden. The privacy of the 'men's stair' was respected, but men who retired to the loft early were often sulking over some incident in the working day, or perhaps burdened by their current love affair, if they were single, or afflicted with some physical disability such as toothache.

'Are you coming down for your supper, Willie?' someone would inquire, and late-coming Willie would lumber down the deal stair looking glum. The effects of love or toothache were extraordinarily similar when both reached the acute stage. I was often given confidences by the men, perhaps because I was a serious-minded child and never laughed at the misery of anyone. Perhaps it was because I didn't ask questions. The confession of being in pain was accepted in silence. 'Willie,' someone would suggest, 'must have fallen out with yon lass he was courting,' but I knew it was nothing of the kind. Willie had an abscess on his gum and he didn't want to tell Grandfather about it or he would be sent off to have the tooth drawn by the travelling dentist, who wasn't really a dentist, and hardly fit to take a tooth from a horse. In due time the abscess would overcome poor Willie's horror of the tooth-puller. Off he would go to the rendezvous where he would spend his odd shilling on enough whisky to numb his jaw and have the tooth dragged out, abscess or no abscess, fractured jaw or not! Strong men they were, all of them.

They came home late from a dance and went to bed in the

small hours to rise again before daybreak to milk, to feed their team and prepare for the day's work. They had their clothes dried after getting wet to the skin and went back out again to work on the back hills, topping and lifting turnips. Sometimes they sat toasting their toes at the fire until their socks steamed regardless of rheumatism, which was the farm labourer's lot. They were willing as well as strong, and asked for very little but a warm bed and a good meal. There was very little else to be had, except so many flannel shirts, so many pairs of socks, so many sets of long drawers and woolly vests, boots and working trousers—and their ten shillings a week, from which would be deducted, come term day, the pocket money they had drawn to buy tobacco or the price of a glass of whisky. 'The best of them didn't need to be called more than once on the coldest, darkest morning and they worked until the day was done, going home to visit their families every other weekend, perhaps, and carrying with them a bundle of dirty washing that would be replaced by laundry from an earlier visit home.

A good man didn't change his place but worked on year after year with the same farmer. A shiftless individual moved about term after term and earned a reputation that did him no credit among prospective employers whose first question would be 'Where were you at before?' Where a man was at was a fair enough yardstick, for one farmer knew what his neighbour demanded of a good man and passed it on to the next. How long a ploughman suffered a hard taskmaster indicated how biddable he was or how lacking in spirit! 'Living-in' ploughmen were a problem in their way, needing to be accommodated in the kitchen and given freedom to run after the lassies or go home when they became suddenly homesick. Cotmen, who lived in the tied cothouse, were a different proposition. They might have families who milked or could be recruited for hoeing the turnips, helping with the hay and the corn harvest. The ploughman and byreman lived in, although now and again, when some peculiarity of their upbringing was discovered, the byreman or the 'boy' might have his quarters in the barn. Here he could sleep with his boots on if he wished and carry out his ablutions when he found the pump water less of a shock than it normally was on a winter's day.

A variety of 'boys' came and went in my childhood. Some of them were old to be called boys. One had been in the army and would drill by himself with a midden brush, sloping and presenting arms to imaginary commanding officers who passed through the byre or shippon and stopped to admire a smartness that the soldier had never displayed in all the time since he had accepted the king's shilling. I used to peer through the cracks of doors to see this conscience-ridden, dishonourably discharged soldier doing his drill. When he discovered me spying upon him he would drop the brush and look at the ground and then begin sweeping the drain or brushing the sets in the stable for all he was worth. We never talked about his failure as a soldier but once he showed me how to use a bayonet and charged a great fat-bellied sack of oats with such vigour that he drove the brush handle through the sacking and grain poured on to the granary floor. We were busy putting it back into the sack when Grandfather appeared on the scene and by some uncanny instinct discovered how the sack had been damaged. The poor soldier found himself mending sacks he hadn't stabbed with the imaginary bayonet! It seemed to me sad that they hadn't taken more trouble to make a soldier of him when they had him in the army. He was a soldier. He marched off, turned corners as he had been taught to turn them, and stamped his foot when he came to a halt, but we wanted more than drill, it seemed, and converting the business of forking sheaves to a one-two-three, he would toss the sheaves farther than they had to be tossed, or pile them up on a stack where the stack-builder would soon become snowed under. 'Yon galoot had all his senses knocked out of him by the sergeant,' the stackbuilder would say, 'if he ever had any senses to begin with!' And the soldier in due time paraded with his kit and went smartly down the road, left-right, left-right, straight-backed, a comic soldier, as useless to the sergeant as he was to us. I suppose I was the only one who understood him. I knew the game he played, the sad make-believe of a man who was still a child and had once gone 'to be a soger' and failed, gay Glengarry with its fluttering ribbons and tartan trews not withstanding.

Another Willie was a poor fellow who hadn't all his wits but had a remarkable memory. He would listen eagerly when Grandfather felt compelled to read some item of news from his paper aloud so that everyone could hear of the event. Daft Willie stored away the account word for word and an hour or so later, perhaps when some member of the family who had missed the event arrived on the scene, Willie would pick up the newspaper and 'read' the item, a feat he performed remarkably well considering that the newspaper could as easily be upside down as sideways. 'Go on Willie,' his audience would urge, but Willie wasn't to be taken out of his depth. He would angrily fold the paper and put it down saying, 'Read the rest for yourselves. What you think I learnt to read for? To let the likes of you make use of me, you ignorant buggers!'

He could write his name when called upon to do so. He wrote laboriously and perspiration might come on his brow as he produced a signature that read from right to left and was legible only if held up to a mirror. Someone had taught him a reasonably safe rule so far as coins of the realm were concerned. He couldn't count, but he knew that any white penny was worth more than a brown one and the larger the white ones were the more they were worth. He knew about sovereigns although no one ever gave him one and his wages were paid over to a relative who bought what he needed and, it was said, put the rest in his pocket. Willie looked after the brood sows and was always greatly concerned to see that they were mated at the right time. Sometimes, for the sake of blood strain this involved Willie acting as a sort of match-maker. Tying a rope to the leg of the sow, and using a stick, he would convey her over the hill to meet her husband, a hairy black boar owned by a neighbour. Willie would come back with a detailed account of the mating and his estimate of the litter that would result when the sow's honeymoon was over, but on one occasion he found one of the sows missing from her pen. She had freed herself by tossing a hurdle with her snout and squeezing out underneath so that she could take the romantic journey without delay. Willie looked about, put his nose to the ground, got up and ran a few paces and got down and sniffed again. He kept up this extraordinary demonstration of his tracking ability as long as he remained in sight and disappeared over the hill hot on the trail of the sow who couldn't wait to be mated. Late in the evening he came back, delighted to inform us that he had tracked her down. Where did we think she was at that very moment? Where but in the very lists of love being served by the black boar!

Grandfather had great compassion for the poor fellow but in the end he had to go after he took a bee in his bonnet and decided he was being persecuted over something he wasn't able to put into words. Poor Willie, time was nothing to him. The sun shone from his countenance for a while and then the clouds would come and he would brood. Sometimes he would insist upon joining in an intelligent conversation and unless he was rebuffed or put in his proper place the excitement of being taken seriously or appearing to have been taken seriously would go to his head and he would talk louder and louder and less and less coherently until froth appeared on his lips. Like the soldier, he went out of my world abruptly. They said he began to wet his bed. He was growing backwards mentally and becoming frighteningly strong physically. Who could say what his end would be? There were many like him in different places, poor demented fellows, the village idiots that couldn't be accommodated in homes and weren't wanted by their relatives. Some of them were gentle with animals and some were prone to violence towards horses and cows and had to be sent away on that account. 'He's not wise,' they would say. It was an under statement but a great deal kinder than calling the poor fellow an imbecile. Like carthorses, such unfortunates are rarely encountered in the country scene these days perhaps because there is less inter-marrying than there used to be, or institutions where the mentally afflicted can be treated may have cleared up the problem that advertised itself on every side in Grandfather's day.

Most of the men we employed came on recommendation from people who knew we needed a man, but now and again it was necessary to advertise for a 'ploughman able to milk' or a byreman who would be expected to look after pigs as well. A procession of applicants would come to 'wage'. It was a ritual rather like buying or selling a horse. For a long time both parties avoided the point at issue and talked about crops and markets and mutual acquaintances, disasters, paternity orders against notorious characters, anything and everything. In the end the suitability of the job or the applicant would be brought into the open. If both sides agreed they would shake hands and a shilling would be given. The shilling was a token of the agreement. It was known as giving a man his 'earls' and the recipient would spit on it and put it into his waistcoat pocket. After this stage had been reached he might be invited to take tea in the kitchen, but if there was any doubt about him this courtesy wouldn't be observed and the family would speculate as to whether he would go home or take the shilling to the nearest public house and buy a dram of whisky with it. When no earls was offered at all it was an indication that although the farmer had shaken hands on the bargain he didn't expect the hired man to show up on the day appointed. If he did show up the earls would be given and the thing forgotten. I quickly came to understand all the delicate nuances of hiring a man or rejecting him without hurting his feelings for I would stand by Grandfather's side and listen to it all and watch the designs he drew on the ground with his walking-stick as he talked. All men weren't alike, nor were they equal, except in the eyes of God. A good man was like a good horse, something to be appreciated and cherished and a lazy man was less use than a bad horse.

14

Doctoring and Curing

Even in the comparatively remote backwaters of Galloway the ordinary and every-day ailments of ordinary every-day children descended upon us. Perhaps the most uncomfortable ailment I suffered was the one that led Jenner to research and inaugurate vaccination. The great man studied the dairymaid's complexion and decided that at a time when the countenance of almost every adult, male or female, of mature age showed the ravages of smallpox it was extraordinary that the milkmaids had comparatively unblemished skins. Poets might talk of the milkmaids bathing in the morning dew but Jenner decided it was more to do with cowpox than the use of dew, or even buttermilk, as aid to beauty. I had been vaccinated as a baby. It didn't prevent me from contracting cowpox but the doctor who treated me for the unpleasant and painful eruptions that the crude vaccine produced was inclined to the opinion that whatever else I contracted in my lifetime I was well protected against smallpox. I was charged with cowpox with a vengeance. I had scratched myself on a nail on which a cow had scratched her hide to relieve the irritation of a sore. I was as unlovely as a victim of the dreaded smallpox, but more fortunate. Cowpox left no permanent pits in the flesh, no blemishes. The scabs hardened and broke away. The agony diminished and I had as much of the untreated, natural serum in my body as it could take. I was resistant to smallpox, that close relative to the cow, if not by blood, by a common strain that had been tested and checked by Mr Jenner when he was on the verge of proving to the world that smallpox need no longer be a scourge.

The treatment of this ailment might well have fallen to Grandfather who had seen all the ailments to which country folk were heir, and had some remedy or recipe for most of them, but my mother, who was alarmed and rightly alarmed at my pathetic state, hauled me off to a doctor in Glasgow so that more expert opinion might be employed. The city doctor could find no cure. Indeed there was no cure. The cowpox had to run its course and my body had to overcome it before I became one vast sore, which of course didn't happen. I remember the pain and the tender parts of my body where I had the sores, but I cannot show evidence of my suffering. The infection left no marks. Denied the chance to cure me of this complaint, Grandfather cured or terminated the last tickling spasms of whooping-cough by taking us, my brothers as well, since they, too, had the complaint and had to be treated, to the King Coast well where we drank the magic water and breathed the intoxicating air and were made whole again. Smile if you must. I firmly believe that most of the weaknesses that show up in the human body are related to the water we drink, to its mineral content, its life, its lack of life, its pollution, its contamination. If you will excuse the word, its particular magic.

The water of the King Coast well, drunk from a seashell, was like no other water I have ever tasted. Like the well from which we used to obtain water when we went on a shore picnic, it was pure, it was sweet, it was cold and it was like champagne. Add to this the fact that we went to take it as a cure on a sun-drenched, summer Sunday when the very air tanned the skin, when the sea was calm and reflected the sunlight away out to the edge of the haze of heat on the water, the bracken gave off a powerful scent, the heather crackled, butterflies flew from one boulder to the next to sun themselves again and again, adders slept in coils and on the shore old men in their black Sunday suits and stiff, shining black boots slept with their hats over their eyes, lying like dead men, careless of life and anything before or to follow that perfect day. We wheezed and coughed and had our minor convulsions of coughing before we went to the well. We climbed the crags and struggled up over boulders, breathed the salty air and the smell of the sun-dried wrack and came at last to the magic well. It was unmarked. Only those who had been taken there on a previous occasion could identify the place and find the little spring. There was a shell close at hand. There had always been a shell there although it was far enough from the beach and the shingle.

Drink, they said. The 'hoast', the tickling cough, the scourge of consumption itself perhaps, might be removed by drinking the water in that place if a man would only drink and believe. A child believed what his elders told him, his grandfather and grandmother, his aunts. Drink, they said, and he drank. Cough no more, they said, gently, sympathetically. Cough no more, for here, today in this place, your cough left you. You drank the magic water and you were cured. No doctor, no medical theory could possibly undo my belief that I was cured there and then that day, long ago. Like religious conviction it is something I need not and will not debate. It is enough to now, to believe, and this I believed in my formative years. No cure is a real cure without faith, without the inner conviction that one is cured, for a man is his mind and his body is only the structure inside which he lives. I came back cured, sunburned, happy. I never forgot the day I went. It stands a milestone in the journey of my life. Had I the same faith in people and things now as I had then I could carry the world on my back!

There was less magic in some of the cures to which I was subjected. Sore throats, common colds, hacking coughs and strains, an obstinacy in their bowels, a thorn deeply imbedded in my hand, a 'bealing'* foot caused by treading on the rusty prongs of a hay fork, all of these ailments had to be doctored. The medicine cupboard contained a variety of things that aren't exactly everyday now: lysol and iodine were commonly used, permanganate of potash, carbolic oil, arnaca, sennapods, sweet nitre, an oil we called 'oil of the night', horse oil, crude molasses that came in big barrels and was fed to cattle along with their ration of hay.

How I loved to get down on my knees and turn on the tap and let the thick black treacle run into my mouth until it almost choked me, and how I paid for this morbid, appetite for days afterwards.

---

* Bealing - festering and inflamed

The two horse plough—Mary on left with Prince on the right.

I would have to leap over a wall or a hedge on the shortest
possible notice to prevent a more serious accident befalling me
than barking my knees on the stones or getting my more tender
parts lacerated by the urgency with which I had to perform what
should have been a natural function but became more frequent
and less natural as the treacle loosened my bowels and churned
me up. 'Have you been at the treacle barrel again?' they would
ask, seeing the almost black streak at the corner of my mouth or
on the end of my nose. Sometimes I denied the charge though
the cock crowed a dozen times. Sometimes I had to admit that
I had been under the tap and they laughed and said I needed a
little sulphur to go with it perhaps. I would never learn that
treacle strong enough for cows was too much for a boy to hold.

I would never learn that green apples were best left to ripen
on the tree and green gooseberries were for making jam and
would never become dessert goosberries like those in old Miss
Dunbar's garden, never in a hundred years. 'The boy needs a
dose of cascara,' Grandfather would say if I happened to look
off colour. I preferred to go out and take a draught from the
treacle barrel if I could escape the cascara bottle. When I had
a cold I would suffer my chest to be rubbed with Elliman's Horse
Oil and would wear a protector in the form of a brown-paper
vest or an old sock tied about my neck, provided I could also
have the standard prescription that Grandfather laid down for
old and young alike, a glass of hot toddy and sugar. I acquired a
taste for toddy but toddy isn't what it was somehow. It never
gives me the glow, the inner warmth, the comfort that
Grandfather's toddy gave me when I was five years old. By the
laws of the bigots I should have been an alcoholic, a whisky
addict at eighteen, but I didn't. The magic went out of the whisky
bottle as steadily as the price went up and I grew older.

When I trod on the rusty hay fork - I went barefoot everywhere
at that time - I said very little about it. In the present day a
doctor would be horrified to think of a boy having such an accident
in a place where horses are numerous without an anti-tetanus
injection being given, but I looked at my foot and limped on until

someone noticed that I had lost some of my fleetness and was extraordinarily reluctant to have my feet examined. By chance I came limping home one afternoon when Grandfather was consulting the vet. What more suitable occasion could there be for surgery than when the vet was there with all his shining tools and bottles of disinfectant were at hand? They invited me to lie on the settle, face downwards and bend my leg so that the sole of my foot could be examined. I had seen what happened to horses. I wasn't keen, to say the least, especially when the vet took out a knife that looked rather like a cut-throat razor and began to look at me as I had seen Grandfather look at young pigs when he was about to 'remove their stones' as he put it. It wasn't the removal of my 'stones' that troubled me, although I would have screamed or squealed to outdo any pig being deprived of its reproductory organs the moment the knife came near me. It was the way two grown men prepared to operate. Grandfather sat down over my thighs without squashing me and gently took hold of my upraised leg, holding the foot so that the vet could come near. The vet dipped his gleaming knife in antiseptic and hissed a little.

'Just in time,' he said. 'Red line running up there, you see?'

I closed my eyes, held my breath, squeezed tears on to my cheeks and felt the knife and the bite of the antiseptic. A bowl of warm water and some cotton wool was handed forward. Grandfather's firm grip was a poor comfort. The bealing foot throbbed and ached. I was sure that the vet was cutting it off or carving away enough of my flesh to leave me a cripple for life - if I lived, which I was sure I wouldn't.

'There's a brave lad,' said the vet when he had done. 'If old Doctor Lillicoe hears about this he'll come round delivering calves to spite me!'

I felt far from brave. They let me up, bandaged my bleeding foot, patted me on the head, gave me a sweet to suck and told me to keep my boots on in future. I limped off, determined to keep my boots on, but equally determined to set off for Glasgow if anyone made as much as one step towards me with a scalpel or lance, or whatever it was they used. I think that the vet put me against doctors, or at least surgeons, for the rest of my life.

A few weeks later, when I was helping with the threshing, or getting in the way of the men who were serving the mill, I felt a pain in my ear. The pain persisted and grew worse. I lay awake at night suffering agony. I could hardly keep my head on the pillow and in the morning when I got up it was plain to everyone that I had something wrong with me. My faith in mankind had been shaken. I would allow no one near me. I dodged and jinked like a rabbit in the corn. I ducked under the table, bolted through the door and took off in my shirt tail for the hills with at least three of the family running after me for all they were worth. I was soon almost completely out of breath and so were my pursuers but I knew that they would catch me and hold me down and perhaps cut off an ear to see where the trouble lay. I stopped and stabbed a finger deep into my swollen and unbearably painful ear, fumbled and poked for a minute and brought out a section of straw sharp at both ends! The pain went. I was in heaven. I could hear the bird singing on the hawthorn tree, the sun was like a fleecy, golden sheep, the clouds were whiter and lighter and like heavenly sailing boats deep in the ocean of the sky. I laughed. They came upon me like bull-baiters. They pounced to bear me off to the doctor or the madhouse, but I laughed. I showed them the piece of straw. I told them it was all over and I wasn't going to die of meningitis or whatever cruel thing had taken the life of my sister Ellen. They stared hard at me, ceased to carry me off like a body-snatcher's plunder, and set me on my feet, kissed and hugged me and said I must have an extra lot of fried scone with my breakfast. I wasn't looking as I should. I must also learn that no one wanted to kill me. All they wanted was to see me fit and healthy.

Drama seemed to come into our lives as naturally as the rain beat on the windows or the sun made the cats bask on the steps. Some years later my brother was walking in the byre when he slipped and fell and rose to find that he could no longer see out of one eye. A gash along the lower eyelid allowed the lid to roll up and it seemed that his eye had gone. Grandfather snatched him from the ground and ran with him to the pump where he douched the wound, and Bob's head, with water, calling loudly in the meantime for the pony to be harnessed and yoked in the gig. Great Aunt Ellen was staying with us. She was pressed into service to hold Bob in her arms. Grandfather drove with one hand and with the fore-finger and thumb of his free hand he held the wound closed. They drove at a break-neck pace all the way to town and at the doctor's house Grandfather raised his voice and boomed to bring the old fellow out. In a minute or two they were in the surgery getting the frightful damage stitched up. Both Grandfather and the doctor did excellent work. The scar that resulted was no more than a hairline beneath the eye.

Not long after this my young cousin, playing round the table at teatime, reached up and pulled a newly filled teapot down over his head. The scream he gave would have shaken the steadiest nerves. There was a moment of panic, perhaps, but not on Grandfather's part. He rose and grabbed a great bowlful of freshly gathered eggs and broke them one after another over the child's head until he was coated with yolks and looked a terrible sight but his pitiful tears abated at last and in due course when the mess of eggs was peeled away he was found to be unmarked despite the fact that he had been in danger of being severely scalded. There was no more damage than brief shock. The eggs were handy but baking soda, bicarbonate, would have served as well although, from the result, no better.

Heal thyself, some would say. Grandfather was his own doctor although his ailments were few and consisted mostly of slight arthritic pains, sore feet and stiff joints, and horse oil seemed to be the cure for these - horse oil and some concoction he obtained from the chemist called Alick o' Pain; but a day came when he was involved in an accident and had to be confined to his bed for several weeks. It happened when he was driving the milk cart, trundling along to the creamery on a bright, frosty morning, his great coat turned up to his ears, his nose buried in his beard, his hands warm in his mittens. All at once the horse, Tammy, began to slide on the hill, took a pace and tripped. Grandfather toppled over the front of the cart and came crashing down on the road. They were on a steep hill and the horse was hard put to it to hold the cart back. Had the cart rolled forward the wheel would have gone over the old man's body, but horses have an instinct for danger of this kind and the horse braced his legs and comforted Grandfather by licking his face with a rasping tongue. They stood there for more than half an hour and then help arrived in the shape of another farmer on his way to the creamery. Grandfather was brought home and put to bed.

He made a terrible patient. Nothing was ever right. His bed was uncomfortable. People closed doors to shut him out of conversations and hide from him things he had a right to know about. He hammered on the floor with his stick and slashed at the waterjug and washbowl and generally made life hell so that half the household was afraid to go down to him and the other half was afraid that he might get out of bed and come storming to the kitchen to give them the full benefit of his thunderous rage.

A week after he had been put to bed he had changed the room, had a pulley screwed through the ceiling into the beams above and tackle rigged so that he could comfortably hoist himself clear of the bed while the pillows, bolsters and so on were being changed or punched up and new sheets spread. He had commandeered every mirror in the house in order to arrange a sort of hall of mirrors enabling him to see right into the kitchen or up the passage and through the door to the court. Doorstops prevented his being frustrated visually and when he couldn't hear what was being said he would demand at the top of his voice that everyone spoke up. The result was that everyone talked as they might have done in a house where everyone was hard of hearing, a habit that puzzled visitors until, out of range of mirrors, a whispered explanation was given and thumbs jerked in the direction of the terror. Understandably Grandfather's recovery didn't take as long as it would have done had he been an ordinary, patient sort of man. He liked chicken broth. One of the reasons everyone was thankful to see him back on his feet was that he insisted on drawing the necks of the doomed birds sitting up in bed and a bedroom isn't the place to have flapping birds and flying feathers, to say nothing of blood.

15

Grass Parks

Philosophers and poets have been saying for a long time that all
life is grass. The animal of the field eats grass. We drink its milk
or eat its flesh. Ashes to ashes or dust to dust, we can only
return to the earth in the end. Life and being, dreams and
daydreams, are quickly short-circuited in this kind of
pronouncement. There is a fair journey to be made through green
pastures between the cradle and the grave and a lot of people
never feel grass beneath the soles of their feet or have any contact
with the elementary, fundamental things of life. Grandfather didn't
look much beyond the hills of Galloway and when he did he looked
for the sun to ripen the corn or make the clover bloom. He looked
at the western horizon to see if rain was coming after he had
harrowed his fields, ploughed and sown them with oats, barley,
rye or ryegrass. When the grass rose, rich and green, it was
pretty soon cropped down again to feed the Ayrshire cows and
the working horses, the stirks and the queys, the store cattle and
the black-faced sheep. The young calves grew and fattened, the
flock multiplied. There was never enough grass. We had to rent
more fields and take stock to wherever those fields happened to
be. For a season or two there would be fields at the Alticry
shore and after that fields on the winding road to the Old Place
of Mochrum. Grandfather and Grandmother had spent a good
part of their lives about the village of Sorbie and they had lived in
Wigtown. It was probably a coincidence, but parks were rented
near Sorbie and below the town of Wigtown, the very fields
Grandfather had rented when he lived in the town and was a
blacksmith there.

Almost any outing turned out to be a great adventure. Going to
a sale was an adventure, going to the market up at Newton

Stewart, attending a cattle show, a ploughing match, or even the creamery run in the morning was an adventure, but taking cattle to the parks was exciting as well as an event of some importance because we were our own drovers. We rounded up the beasts that were to be moved, had our dinner and set out to herd the young bullocks, calves and the rest, along the public road. There was no other way. Cars weren't too numerous on the roads of Wigtownshire, even when I was in my early teens, but when I was a small boy motor cars travelled with extra caution. The roads still belonged to the men who had made them, the drovers of cattle, the farmers who travelled from one field to the next and knew what roads were for and who had most right to be on them! When I was small I journeyed in the gig which generally brought up the rear. Someone went in front with a collie dog or two, and one or two others chivvied the bullocks along and saw that they kept to the route without breaking through into adjoining fields, thrusting their way through gates or leaping over low hedges or drystone walls. It was a business that had to be done at a pace suitable to the stock. It was no use hurrying the cattle along until they were exhausted and stood with their sides heaving, soiling the road. That kind of cruelty no one would allow and the old man in the gig would have been the first to raise his voice had anyone attempted to hurry. I think this was why I liked the journey to the grass parks so much. We travelled as country folk loved to travel, without haste, looking about us, exchanging the time of day with the people we met, thanking the cothouse folk for herding the bullocks back out of their potato patch without scowling at us for the damage they might have done. There was time to stop and talk. Grandfather loved to talk to his neighbours. He had a fund of knowledge about the countryside and the people who lived in it. Even people he didn't know he could quickly identify by inquiring who their father was, or where they had been born. While the bullocks ambled on, pulling grass from the verges or corn from a field close to the wall, he would indulge in his favourite game of showing people how familiar he was with their whole lineage.

'Ah,' he would say, 'I know you fine. Your mother was from up about New Luce. Her mother was old Nan Williamson. I see the likeness in you. You'll be married to Tam Murphy from Monreith, brother to Mick from Drumorea' And he would be off through a great network of related families, coming back down through them all again to inquire if the woman had any children, how many she had, their ages, and were they all living? By that time the bullocks would be out of sight behind a hill and on we would trundle to supervise once again until we came upon someone else, old Harry the stone-breaker perched on his great mountain of boulders in the roadside quarry, or a tinker on his way from one village to the next. 'You'll be a Kyle?' the old man would say and the tinker would smile and admit to the name. The Kyles had been here and there and everywhere. Their crimes were known. Their bastard children were without number. Grandfather knew when to be tactful, when to make a joke and bid the tinkers good day and go on. Over in the croft lived old Bob in the Whins, a sort of hermit whose contact with the world was slight though he loved to stand and stare at anyone passing his road end. We waved to old Bob in the Whins, but he rarely acknowledged that he had seen our greeting. He had counted the bullocks, no doubt, and knew just what stock was going to the grass park.

Perhaps one of the droving party would miss an open gate and the leading heifer would plunge into a hayfield, taking all the rest with her in a wild, abandoned stampede, and we were suddenly in dire trouble, or a particularly wayward or amorous beast would break away from the rest and make a cross-country rush for freedom. One black Galloway in a herd of black Galloways looks very like another! The owner of the beast might be able to tell his own, but sometimes even he would be in some doubt. The only reliable mark was the ear-clip. 'Dammit to hell!' Grandfather would shout, 'look what's happened us now!' The dogs would race over those strange, bottomless, unfamiliar pastures. The order we had known would all at once become chaos. We needed all the help we could muster to bring back the stray. In the meantime, the rest of the beasts were free to go on or turn back to explore the ditches and escape into fields we knew nothing about.

The dismay we felt at having to hunt down a single stray was nothing to the dismay we knew when the untended herd got into a field of corn or raced through young turnips, thinning them out more effectively than any man with a hoe could have done! The owner of the field would tear his hair at the sight of the damage and it wouldn't take him long to know who was responsible. News travels as fast in the quiet countryside as it does anywhere else. The very infrequency of social contact ensures this. With any luck however, we would recover the heifers and get them back on the road, heading in the right direction, without having done too much damage, and the cyclists would wobble and sway, riding very slowly to see that the beasts were kept moving just fast enough to overcome their tendency to explore without making them stampede again.

The last half mile or so was always exciting for soon we would have the herd safely shut in one of the parks. The novelty of droving had long since worn off. Grandfather had had his 'crack' with all the worthies and characters along the way, and had looked more than once at his watch, thinking about the milking that would have to be done by those who had helped move the stock. I loved to see the way animals that had been to a particular park before quickened their pace as though they were as aware as we were that the journey was at an end and soon they would graze on familiar ground. The dogs would see them to the open gate. Without being driven the cattle would break into a run and kick up their heels and swing their tails as the gate was fastened. It was good to see them going to drink or hurrying to join the stock we had brought there a month or two before. It was good to see so much rich grass and know that now there would be enough for the animals on the home fields.

'Ah well,' the old man would say, 'we've got them to the parks safe and sound. Now haste you back and get the milking done.'

The pony would whirl the gig round in the road and his forefeet make a rapid tattoo as he ran. The wind would be in our faces, the pestilential flies left behind. We sang, smelt the honeysuckle, the cottage roses. Even the tang of a field of swedes in summer has something special about it. Dogs would be barking milking-herds home from the pastures as we hurried along. The cyclists would be long out of sight. If we had no other excuse for haste we were hungry. Our mouths watered at the thought of scones and a wedge of strong red cheese, hot, butter-melting oven scones brought out from beneath a floury cloth, wood-smoked tea, or just bread and butter and a big, double-yolked egg.

There were times between taking animals to the parks and bringing them back again—for they didn't stay there indefinitely—when we had to visit these places to look them over, count the heads and see that none was sick. This was another pleasant excursion. I loved to accompany the old man on this trip and go down with him into those strange fields where the cattle were grazing. Fields always seemed vast, wonderful places to me as a child. I studied the topography of them, loved the little knolls, the stone-heaps, the gorse patches, the damp corners where round rushes or flags grew. I loved great seas of clover and the sight of Scotch thistles in seed with goldfinches upon them, and stands of rusty dock and yellow-and-green forests of ragwort that sometimes sheltered a hare or a skulking pheasant. I loved the less familiar grass parks because they were less familiar and therefore more mysterious and in need of exploration. Even the waterholes and the waterhens that frequented them were strangely more exciting than the waterholes and waterbirds I knew at home. The bullocks had changed, too, by living in the strange, distant world to which we had driven them. I doubt whether Grandfather felt as I did or knew how these places affected me, for a child's world and a man's world are quite different. A dock was an ugly thing to him, a thistle, a sign of a lazy farmer. He saw no beauty in a sea of charlock, or in the red-andwhite flowers of the weeds in the turnip rows. At the parks he stood and considered the business of renting pasture and whether or not he had profited by doing so. The grass was meat to the thick-coated Galloway calves. When they had cropped it all they would come out of the field and leave it to the spreading weeds they wouldn't eat, the harebells, vetch and yarrow, and the purple blossomed knapweed.

At home we cropped the fields in a three-year rotation. So many acres of corn and then a change to roots and back to corn and then fallow again while new pastures were ploughed under. Some of the fields were sown with grass to be cropped in hay and some provided a crop of wild hay, bog hay, and round rushes for thatching at harvest time. Hardest on the pasture were the hungry sheep that left the places between the whins as trim as the minister's lawn and then searched the boundary for a breaking-out place. Black-faced sheep are notorious for this kind of wandering. Bred in them is a nomadic urge to explore, to graze the whole of the pasture under the open sky, and this they will contrive to do wherever they come to a wall or a fence, or even a ditch. Perhaps we were overstocked or it may have been that there was some miscalculation in the use of the acreage. Some people didn't go in for grass parks, as far as I knew, and some people had more grazing than they needed, or we should never have been able to rent the parks.

When the stock had to be brought home because the grass was exhausted, or the tenancy was up, or simply because the beasts had to be sheltered and fed standing in over winter, we gathered our forces and went back to round them up. Once, I remember, we went to town and combined a visit to the circus with a visit to the parks. What a day that was! The rain dripped through the circus tent. The atmosphere was damp, the plank seats soiled and wet, and we were wet ourselves, but we admired the lumbering elephant and the old monkeys with their fleapicking habits, the moulting parrots and colourful, impudent macaws, for we knew animals. They belonged in our world. We thought less of the horses for they, poor beasts, were made to look foolish performing humiliating tricks. Afterwards we went out into the rain, rounded up our own circus, and took to the road. They were no longer Galloways and Ayrshires, but elephants, buffaloes and the other creatures we had seen in the circus menagerie. We were performers ourselves, with an audience of countryfolk on their way home. The byreboy was a trick cyclist, the collie dogs were wolves, no less, and the ringmaster rode behind. I doubt if the cattle were really aware of the role they were supposed to be playing. They jogged into the rain without troubling to deviate from their proper path. They were on the way home. They knew where they were going, for cattle, like sheep, belong in the place on which they are reared. They never lose a homing instinct unless they have been kept away for a long time.

It wasn't quite by chance that excursions of this sort often fell on wet days. The time best suited to droving was when most of us were prevented from doing things we normally did out of doors. Grandfather studied the signs and decided that on such and such a day we would move the stock. The bulk of the younger animals went in the company of at least one beast that had made the journey before. Droving is made easier when the lead beast knows the way. Only occasionally would droving be done in the middle of a dry spell when the grass had to be conserved. To embark on such adventure on a fine summer's morn was everything we could hope for. The whole world was wonderful: the rooks flew high, the river wound bright and shining through the water-meadows, cattle in the roadside fields lumbered along in order to keep us company as far as the dividing walls would allow. Even the heifers and bullocks seemed to smell the breeze and enjoy the journey.

Alas, such days were few and far between and it was too often a trip for which we were decked out in oilskins with the rain in our faces. To go was to come back again, however. To know the cold and the rain was to appreciate the comfort of home. Everything physical is best appreciated by contrast. I loved to come back again to the kitchen on a wet afternoon and feel the warmth of the big iron range as my wet clothes were dried and enjoy the sight of those hearth cats crowding each other inside the fender, sleeping until supper time. Sometimes, it is true, I thought about the stock we had left behind in those rain-swept, far-away parks, standing with their backs to the dripping hedge and ruminating on the grass they had munched. Grandfather, if he gave them another thought, probably took another mental measure of the amount of 'keep' they had, and how long it would be before he brought them back again. He had no time for sentimental dreams. Grass was milk, scones on the girdle, meat on our plates, clothes on our backs, a roof over our heads. I doubt whether he had ever heard, or read, that all life is grass.

16

Rain - Gentle and Un-gentle

That Galloway gets its fair share of rain no one would deny. There never was good dairy-farming country that didn't. It rained when I was a small boy, as it rains now, and I am glad that the nostalgia from which I suffer includes recollections of wet days, rain on the skylight, rain sighing over a barley field, sweeping like a curtain right across from the Atlantic, falling on our backs in great droplets bigger than a shilling the minute we stepped into the hayfield, dancing in the puddles of the road, following the wild duck and the curlew into the haze at nightfall. Wet days in plenty troubled those who had work to do, but they didn't trouble a child overmuch when he could watch the ducks leaving the gig house and taking a shower where the corrugated iron of the shed poured a deluge on the stony ground beneath. They loved the rain for they belonged in the wet and their delight was a laughable contrast to the dejection and misery of almost every other creature, the horse with his rear end turned towards the rain, the wet and bedraggled fowls that roosted on spars and preened their 'drook-ed' feathers and looked like bundles of wet rag. Out to the burn went the ducks without anyone to say them nay, and out to the burn I would go too, if I could slip away to sail a boat or wade the spate and watch the ducks swim on under the road and into the tunnels of over-hanging grass and dripping hawthorns and broom bushes.

'It's a wet one,' someone would say, stamping his feet to shake rain from his clothes and batting his old tweed cap against the lime-washed wall of the stable, cursing the weather that delayed hay-making or some such urgent duty. The heron fished in the rain and along the shelter of the hedgeside the hare loped and grazed and peewits flew from one water-logged field to the next.

Out of the mist came the cormorants crossing land between bays and swimming in the air almost as easily and gracefully as they did in deep water after fish.

When I discovered how to fish and learned that spate brought out the biggest trout to feed I came to love the rain. I would deck myself in oilskin coat and hat and take myself off to fish in the burn, and the burn the ditch ran to, and the river that the burn fed . . . on into the magic world of gliding water and trailing weed and inundated round rushes where the rain sizzled down and crept along stalks and pattered on the riverside waterlilies. Over my boot-heads I would go, they said, and come home with wet feet and that was bad enough, but I might find myself in deeper water and sail away to the sea with the ricks that the flood picked up in the watermeadows and dead old trees and gates and barrels and chicken coops. They were often angry with me for the fright I gave them when I managed to slip away in the rain. Was it not enough that clothes had to be dried for men who had been drenched at work, not enough that ducks and ducklings had to be shepherded back and the floor of the kitchen washed a score of times to remove the pattern of mud and wet boots? The dogs stayed at home in the rain. Rain was for the wild duck and the scarts* and herons.

A boy had no business to be out when the burn had a froth on it like a glass of stout and the fording places were lost and everything went gliding away, sleek and dangerous as an adder in the long grass. There were stories by the score of people drowning in ditches that normally wouldn't come up to a man's knees and carts going over into holes that swallowed them and trapped the man sitting on the fore-end. In the long glides I caught trout. In the places where there were big stones I caught trout. In holes under walls where the water lapped and even out among the round rushes normally yards from the burn, I caught fish, but it wasn't just that I could fish. I loved the rain in my face. I loved to see the burn rise and the way debris, leaves, feathers of duck and other waterfowl spun in a whirlpool and slowly turned in some backwater. I loved to hear the water thundering beneath

---

* Scart a local name for cormorant, thought to be a corruption of the Icelandic name of the bird, 'Skafr'.

the bridge and see some fragment of a dead, bleached tree slowly trundled through the rocks, gaining a yard or two on its journey of a year or two, heading slowly towards the estuary and the sea.

The sun shone through the rain. I loved the drama of the rain-clouded sky full of great black monsters about to unload gallons of water on the fields, just as I loved the spouting roadside drains, the puddles joining one another to make a roadside stream and then disappearing. Grandfather himself was little troubled by the rain but he had to make sure that I didn't catch a chill, didn't go in over my head and finish up a corpse, and out he would come to 'cry' me home, to thunder at the top of his voice in every direction to bid me return from whatever wet corner of the place I was lurking in. When I heard this alarm my heart would sink. I would hide myself, putting off the moment when we would meet and I would face his wrath, which rarely improved with keeping. I was going to drown trying to catch a little trout, seeing if I could still wade the drinking hole down at the corner of the old stackyard field. I was going to drown in the Malzie Burn. It would serve me right!

That I didn't drown in the smithy burn or catch my death through getting drenched to the skin was remarkable. I was often tempted to drink from the spate and more than once I tested its depth where it ran to brim in a culvert under the road piling up fern and bracken and grass and bits of stick from the thorn hedges, and I would go out along the burns to set lines for trout, putting pegs not unlike snare pins in the bank and throwing a line into the burn with a hook and a worm at the end of it. Having set the lines I could hardly wait to go back and look at them and many a fine lusty trout I took, monsters of half a pound and even three-quarters, golden, redspotted, fat fish the like of which I have never caught again for all the fine tackle I possess and all the big trout I have brought to my net, for these fish came from the magic waters of my childhood. They swam in the deeps among waving grass and undulating weeds and they took my midden worm and stayed there, moored until I came again to haul them out. Every one was a fish that was enchanted, marked with rubies and glowing like precious metal, coloured as nothing else was coloured, by enchantment. I would bring these fish home and have them for breakfast just as I brought home the eggs of the peewit and ate them in season, but the magic was in the rain, away in the secret parts of the burn, the wellwashed stones, the slabs, the boulders and the overhanging bushes.

'Dammit to hell! Where in blazes have you been until this time?' Grandfather would demand, his stick thudding into the ground, his eyes flashing fire, his rage like the start of a thunderstorm. 'Am I to write to your father and tell him you are drowned in the burn?'

But I wasn't drowned in the burn and had never been, for here I was to prove it, carrying four or five precious golden trout on a withy stick and determined not to come back to the world of wet socks and steaming clothes and raging grandfathers if I could keep my ears closed and my mind where it loved to be, as far away from reality as it could be, rain or shine.

'I'll have no more of it! Back you'll go to your father and see what he can make of you!'

How my heart sank when these words penetrated to my running-away mind. I stood still in the long green tunneis and in the magic waters and saw the dark demons waiting for me in the town, in the black caverns where cigar smoke and electrical flash and roar of tramcars took the place of everything in my enchanted world.

I was never banished, never reported for my misdemeanours, for I suppose they saw how things were with me, but I would lie awake listening to the rain drumming on the skylight and dancing on the tin roof of the back porch and include in my prayers a special request to God not to have me transported to the long gulleys of wet streets and the cliffs of endless shops and tenements, for I had seen them once.

The wet days that so delighted me when I learned to fish were none the less delightful when I couldn't fish but found myself on a journey to the market or the town, huddled down in oilskins and watching the river growing as we drove alongside it, seeing the people of the village back inside their cottages with their curling-stone doorstops keeping the doors against the wall. The cottages were all prone to damp and it was fatal to keep the doors closed on muggy, wet days in summer. All enjoyment depends on contrast, the enjoyment of warmth by first being cold, the enjoyment of being dry by first being wet, the enjoyment of rain on one's skin by having a parched, hot, dry skin. The gentle rain would reduce the hay to a sort of mouldering compost, bleach the sheaves and grow grass on an old stack thatch. The un-gentle rain would drive under the kitchen door so that a mat or a strip of sacking had to be placed along the doorstep to absorb the flood. The un-gentle rain would sting our faces as we rode home from the creamery and make the plodding horse turn his head to one side and go slower. It flooded the midden and made sure that the spring beneath the pump never went dry. It overbrimmed the rain barrel and the gutters and dripped steadily from the eaves of stable and byre and cartshed, while the hollows in the meadows filled up and waterfowl swept in to feed and paddle and take off again. Everyone kept his eye on these special places. When they began to dry the drains were taking the flood away and the land was fit to be worked. When they rose it was obvious that the sheaves were going to sprout and the rising aftergrowth would fasten them to the ground and the result would be spoilt corn and a poor, a ruinous harvest. It didn't only rain in February. It rained for a good part of the year. If it fattened carrots and turnips it also flattened acres of growing corn and stopped all work outside.

There were days when I didn't go to the burn and days when the venturesome ducks came hurrying back, twitching their tails because the rain was cold and the wind even colder. I would go in search of the men and find them in the barn, in the granary, in the stable. In their company I received a particular sort of education, all the myths and legends, the fanciful stories of the country-side. No wonder I believed in ghosts, in fairies, in charms and curses, strong men and demon horses. There was a special snugness in the warm, dry stable with its smell of horses and leather, especially when rain swept through the steading. The door was generally left ajar for the men liked to keep one eye open for the 'maister'. Their comparative privacy would be now and then encroached upon by inquisitive fowls that cocked their heads and nervously stalked in to pick grain from the manure in the stalls. Sometimes the door was closed. It was a folding-door and when it was closed the stable was very private and rather dark for the cob-webbed skylight up in the rafters admitted little daylight. The sliding-shutters above the corn chest were shut to keep out the draught and the driving rain. So long as one corner of the stable wasn't packed to the roof with straw for bedding the men smoked and talked or sang while one of them played the mouth-organ. They drummed their heels on the corn chest and cursed the weather for they were generally industrious and found it irksome to have nothing to do. Now and again, despite the downpour, a cockerel standing in the entrance to one of the sheds or out-buildings would crow, and someone would remark that the cloud was lifting. Cocks crowed at the clearing of the sky. It would be a clear evening, wait and see, with the flooded river shining in the sunlight and those big, muddy-looking clouds gone right out over the far hills.

Like the men, Grandfather found something disturbing in the mere thought of idleness. He was probably a slave-driver. Most farmers at that time had to drive hard to make ends meet. He would come to the stable to see if he could find some sort of work to occupy his men. The chaff house might be emptied, the cartshed tidied, the calf house cleaned, the barn floor scraped, pigs re-bedded, harness sorted, sacks repaired. Once in a while he set the men to making a variety of ropes with a ropeweaving device he had invented, a piece of equipment that made use of lengths of binder twine to make plough lines, ropes for tarpaulin sheets and draught ropes. It was a business that required supervision and took a considerable amount of time, in consequence of which it was never embarked upon unless the weather had been carefully checked. It was no use beginning to make a rope and then abandoning the project when the sun came out and in any case a damp atmosphere was essential for the weaving of the sisal. I was fascinated to see them making ropes, which they did on the byre walk, the only building with the length necessary for the purpose. Sometimes I had visions of even longer ropes being made by the same process in great long buildings covering miles of bricked floor. I was disappointed to learn that machines did the job faster, although not any better.

Making ropes was a limited sort of occupation since only so many ropes were needed even when unthatched ricks were sheeted, and all the carts and ploughs and plough teams had to be supplied. If nothing else could be found for him to do a man might be sent out to cut thistles, muffled up to the nose in oilskins, but this was a sort of a punishment. He could also be sent to the distillery for bran on a wet day, so long as he didn't stop to get drunk, not at the distillery, of course, for there the hawk-eye of the exciseman and the bonding department prevented anyone from helping himself, but at the public house just across the way. Even those who didn't drink seemed to get a little intoxicated at the distillery. Perhaps the heady air, the spirit atmosphere of the place was enough, and a man got drunk simply breathing the fume. I sometimes went to the distillery and stood watching the bran being shovelled into the cart. It had the 'distillery smell' about it. Our pigs loved the stuff and grew fat upon it for it was the residue of the malting barley. When the cart was full to overflowing with the wet mess of bran I would be lifted up on to the fore-end and sit there while the load was taken home, uphill and down dale, jolting and swaying in the rain. I was never aware of haste and never in danger of falling off backwards into the bran, as Uncle Peter had done one fateful day when he had been sampling some of the distillery's output.

Home I would come, looking like a 'drook-ed crow', my face red and my cheeks wet with rain, my appetite more ravenous than ever. What would my mother think of me if she could see me now they would ask. I looked like an orphan of the storm, the shepherd's son from some wild and remote corner of the moors.

What indeed, would my town-bred mother say when the thinnest veneer of gentility I had acquired was all worn off and the peasant had taken possession of me? Even my father, who must have known that I didn't sit in the parlour eating biscuits all day, would have been disturbed to hear what I knew about bastardy and adultery before I could recite the alphabet. Rain falls on the wicked and the innocent. I learned a great deal on wet days! On dry days everyone had too much work to do to dally talking.

17

Off on Holiday

Holidays, I am inclined to think, were like being married in
church, which, after all, was only Christian and proper, but, like
being married, with full ceremony and the bride in white, an
occasion in a lifetime! I am sure the few brief and far-between
holidays my grandparents took troubled their consciences when
they took them, for they were bound to their tasks with leg-irons,
with chains. They saw the corn growing, the blossom changing
on the potato rows, the aftergrowth coming on the desolated
hayfield, the young rushes rising where they had been scythed,
calves and sheep fattening and, perhaps, the elm trees beyond
the midden, their ageing perceptible only to their keen eyes. They
were part of the place. Everyone was, of course. There was a
derision in the inquiry when one asked the other, 'When are you
off on your holidays, then?' It sometimes indicated that someone
was leaning overhard on a hayrake or a fork. Sometimes one of
the family would set off to tackle a particularly gigantic task
with the comment that they were off on their holidays.

Holidays were a dream in reality indulged in by those who
worked in cities and thought that they had done a day's work
when they got out of bed at seven in the morning and ended their
labours at five or six in the evening. Holidays were for
schoolmasters and work-shy devils who contrived to find the
easy way of living, for ministers, God forgive us, for those with
soft palms and corpulent shape, the grasshoppers of the world,
and those who would always manage to lie in the sun! It befitted
everyone to have a holiday perhaps once or twice in his life,
however, so that they could say they had provoked fate and left
everything and gone, walked the hard pavements of the city and
stared over bridges and got in the way of women pushing prams

while they stared upwards at some great novelty that was no
novelty at all to those who saw it every day. To be dressed in
one's best and to do nothing—like the laird who sat in one room
smoking his pipe all morning and moved into another to smoke
his pipe in the afternoon because some tiresome woman had to
tidy the place up, like the minister who walked with his hands
behind his back from Monday until Sunday, 'working' at the
subject of hell and damnation, when he was already in heaven.
So it seemed. I may be wrong, and those who were blessed with
a holiday may have found it irksome and were thankful that they
didn't have time on their hands like the useless people they
encountered in the town.

Grandmother and Grandfather didn't take a holiday that I can
remember during the time I lived there, but later on, soon after
we had moved south to London, my father persuaded them that
they should come and stay with us and enjoy seeing things they
had always wanted to see; and they came south at last, dressed
in their best, he a broad, limping giant of a man and she a neat
little white-haired countrywoman with all the dignity of a queen.
They brought an air of the country with them, a suggestion of
peat smoke. A haunting sound of the curlew calling that not
everyone could detect, came with them too. The sun went down
in the flat country of Middlesex and in the cloud shadows I saw
the hills, the pine trees and the corner of the garden, the smoky
horizon away beyond the moors. Sheep-dogs barked and
swallows twittered in the rafters of the far-away cartshed. I
don't think the old people saw these things. They had no nostalgia
choking them. They were unsentimental about the country from
which they had journeyed. They had no need to be sentimental
when tomorrow they could turn about and go back again.
Grandfather wanted to see almost everything that was to be seen,
the roads the drovers took to Smithfield, the places where the
highwaymen robbed their victims, the Tyburn tree upon which
they were hanged, monuments and cathedrals, castles and
dungeons, regalia, pageants and parades. He also wanted to see
what the city-dweller grew in his little garden and how he grew

it without good manure,with all that soot falling upon his head and such poor soil around his feet. He walked countless miles in search of all the attractions he had come to see, emerging from the underground and taking his watch from his pocket and standing to ponder where the sun was before he found his bearings. My father plodded behind and wondered if he hadn't taken on an impossible task.

I treasured a dream during this memorable holiday, a forlorn hope that they would take me back home, for I hated the flat country and the clay fields and the canals, the dreary mounds that passed for hills and the dull, lumbering Shire horses that pulled the brewers' carts and looked as though they had never seen a field of lush green grass or breathed air other than the air of the streets. There were curlews flying over London. Grandfather stopped in the busy street and listened to one and I heard it too. It didn't make me love the city, but it pained me for I was sick with longing to be back where the curlew rightfully belonged. My father knew this well enough. On a brief visit to his native countryside he had brought back three pigeons from the ridge of the barn so that I could be reunited with them and he spent a considerable amount of time and labour housing these undistinguished homingbirds in a sort of pigeon-loft-cum-rabbit-hutch. It wasn't his fault that I had to let them out to fly round. They didn't return but it was surely remarkable that one of them found its way back to the farm and was identifled quite positively. It had the same desperate longing to return to the place in which it had been reared that I had. Everyday of that holiday I prayed inwardly to be taken back. It wasn't to be.

Grandfather showed as much interest in the Thames as he took in the other, more spectacular sights he demanded to be shown. The river, it was explained, was controlled by weirs, but this didn't convince him that it wasn't going to break its banks and flood part of Chelsea. He made this prediction one afternoon while plodding along the Embankment with father at his side. My father was a thoroughly practical man with a great respect for engineers of every kind. He took off his hat to the builders of bridges and dams, to those who built towers and drove tunnels. He had given a lot of his own time to engineering subjects and knew something of the mystery of the internal combustion engine, the principles of construction in steel, the characteristics of alloys, the power of hydraulics. He felt compelled to give his father a sermon on the wide subject of engineering and mathematics, and he did. The Thames could not break its banks because precautions were taken to see that this could never happen. The experts knew precisely how much the river would rise or could rise, in any set of circumstances. It was as straight-forward as controlling a water hole in a pasture. To ensure the public safety everything that was done involved an extra factor to make special allowance for all the freakishness of nature. It could not happen. It was foolish talk to suggest that it could!

Grandfather put away his watch and said it was time to go home for tea. He had had enough. He was weary of the hard pavements. The sights had palled. He had seen the Changing of the Guard and the ravens on the Tower of London. The bridge had opened and closed for him. The traffic at the Bank was as bewildering as bees swarming or the work of ants inside an anthill. He was going home to rest his head in peace on a chaff pillow, far away from the noise and the smoke and the foul smell of the underground. Tomorrow night, no matter what father said, no matter how clever the engineers were, and all the built-in safety they could devise, the river would rise and the Thames would overflow the embankment and people in Chelsea would drown. Why would this happen? It would happen because, standing there on the Embankment, Grandfather had seen it happen. He had seen the great brown river lapping the stones and rising minute by minute. He had seen it running into basements and cellars and heard the cries of those who were trapped. Laugh if you like and talk about science. There was more in the world than buildings in stone or steel and calculations on graph paper, slide rules and formulae. There was vision, the thing old Nan the Witch had had, the thing that could be dulled in one generation but was bright in another. They said very little more to each other all the

147

way home. Grandfather looked out at the black walls of the underground tunnels and closed his mind to the racket and the clatter of the train. He was as sure of his vision as he was of the sun rising and setting. No matter what arguments my father might put forward what he had seen he had seen and it would surely happen. Grandmother knew that he was right. My mother knew that my father was right. They avoided argument. Father smiled an amused smile and felt a great warmth towards his father because the old man was a simple countryman and didn't know what he was talking about. Grandfather didn't smile. He was thinking about the people in Chelsea and the fate that would surely befall them.

The following morning while Grandmother packed their things for the journey Grandfather went out to buy my father a spade. I went with him. He told me about the impending disaster as we went along to the ironmonger's shop. I knew it would happen. We went into the ironmonger's and stated our requirements or at least Grandfather told me in the quick broad speech of Galloway what I had to say to the ironmonger and I played interpreter, although there was no need to tell Grandfather what the ironmonger was saying. He could translate for himself. He wasn't at all baffled by the English accent.

'Tell him this is a no-use, hopeless thing and a spade is a spade,' said Grandfather, thrusting the condemned spade into my hands. I flushed a little.

'We would like to see a different kind of spade,' I said as gently as I could.

The ironmonger was a dwarf of a man. He looked up at Grandfather like David facing Goliath and at any minute it seemed to me he would reach into his little hip pocket and bring out a slingshot, but he didn't. He found another spade with which Grandfather turned imaginary turves and seemed about to throw the spade down in disgust when he remembered again where he was and what he was doing.

'Tell him nobody could dig the ground with this kind of straight spade. It's made for leaning on!'

148

'My grandfather wants a spade a bit better than this one,' I said.

The ironmonger scowled and went off to rummage among a forest of spades and each one was discarded until Grandfather found one that was balanced and came well to the hand. He dug a small pit in the floor with it and smiled through his beard at the dwarf.

'Tell him this is the right thing and ask him what in blazes kept him from offering me this spade in the first place? Do I look like an amateur, a man who never had sweat on his brow?'

'My grandfather is pleased with this spade,' I told the little man who took the spade from the giant and carefully wrapped the blade in brown paper.

'Will there be anything else?' he inquired.

'One thing at a time,' said Grandfather without the help of his interpreter, 'but I'll tell you something, little fellow, tomorrow night they'll have a great spate on the Thames and people with be drowned along the Embankment.'

The dwarf shook his head and rang up the till and gave us our change. Quite plainly he thought that the foreigner was quite mad and had been rashly let out with only a child for company! We went back home with the spade and in the afternoon Father and Mother took Grandfather and Grandmother to Euston to catch the night train.

I told my father what Grandfather had said in the ironmonger's shop and he was highly amused until we came to the prediction of disaster. This kind of nonsense was all very well inside the family but I wasn't to go about telling people my grandfather said such things. It reflected on his sanity—and mine! Mother whispered to me to be quiet and not spoil our leave-taking by prompting a discussion on the subject of the Thames overflowing. I didn't need to. Grandfather patted my head and Grandmother kissed my cheeks and said she would take me back if only my father and mother could be persuaded to part with me. I looked at the roof of the station and the sooty sparrows there and wished that I were dead.

'Well boy,' said Grandfather, 'you'll look after them all and be thankful that you don't live near the water.'

'I will,' said my father as they shook hands solemnly.

The engine rumbled and stopped jetting steam on to the platform. The whistle blew and the coaches began to roll away. I squeezed the tears from my eyes and held my mother's hand as we went back to the underground. I hadn't felt the need to hold her hand for a long time. It was dark when we reached home. I went to bed thinking of my grandfather sitting in the railway carriage smoking his black twist and frowning at his vision of the Thames in flood. In the morning my father opened his newspaper to find the front page filled with the story of the Thames breaking its banks somewhere in the region of Chelsea. I don't remember now how many people were drowned.

'My God!' said Father, 'he saw it before it happened. He was right and I was wrong!'

My mother whose highland ancestry could never be subdued sat in horror as the account was read to her. I listened and said nothing. They looked at me and I was tempted to ask if I might go along the road to the ironmonger's shop and jog the dwarf's memory.

'We were here yesterday, buying a spade,' I would say, 'and you thought me and my grandfather mad. You looked on him as a simple country fellow who couldn't count his fingers. You raised your little eyebrows when he told you about the Thames and people being drowned. Are you smiling now? Are we as mad as you thought we were? We see tomorrow. My great-great-grandmother was Nan the Witch. She could put a curse on all your spades and a hump on your back for good measure!'

How I wanted to go there and say those things! My father looked up and caught my eye.

'You'll say nothing to anybody about this,' he warned.

'People would think you and Grandfather were liars anyway, if they didn't say he was mad!'

'But it happened,' I said, 'and he didn't say it afterwards. He said it before it happened and he said it to you and me and the ironmonger.'

Mother got up and patted my head. 'Never mind,' she said. 'A lot of people say a lot of things and a lot of people don't believe them.'

'You'll write to Grandfather and tell him that it happened?' I asked.

'He knows it happened,' my father said. 'He knows, but I'll tell him I believe he saw it.'

In due course my father wrote and told Grandfather that he had convinced him there was more in the world than science and raw material. There was such a thing as second sight, and Nan the Witch lived in us yet. Grandfather himself told the story for a long time afterwards and told it without gloating about the fact that he had been right, but there had been many occasions in his life when he had had visions of the sort and they had come about as he had predicted they would.

One day, long afterwards, I went into the ironmonger's shop and spoke to the little man about Grandfather and the spades. He had forgotten what we had come in to buy. He remembered the prediction. He stood and looked hard at me.

'Thought you and your old grandad was a pair,' he said. 'Told the wife about you. Told her what the old fellow said but not until next morning when I read it in the paper. You tell your grandad he could make his fortune. You tell him to think about horses and see what's going to win!'

I should have liked to have told Grandfather about the little fellow, but it wasn't possible, for by that time Grandfather and Grandmother were both in their graves. It would be fitting in a way if I could prove that I have a similar gift and demonstrate that Nan the Witch, who lived in Grandfather, lives in me too, but I have no such power. I have never seen the future, charmed a horse or cursed anyone or anything with satisfactory result, which is probably just as well. Not everyone can live with such power. I doubt whether I could see tomorrow and live through today.

18

Journey to the Cemetery

It seems to a child that the world stands still, especially if he is happy. His parents and his relatives live for ever and hardly grow older at all. So it had seemed to me, although I must admit that I never thought about it until long after my grandmother was dead. I was thirteen years old. I had once watched a funeral with plumed horses and a band with crepe-muffled drums playing the Dead March, but that had been a sort of pageant and any connection with death I didn't really understand. I remember my grandmother's face in death as I remember with anguish the faces of my father, mother and grandfather when they, too, were lying still for ever with their eyes closed. Grandmother's death image is like a monument in my recollection of childhood. She was the first person who had ever died so far as I was concerned. When I saw her in her coffin and kissed her cold cheek I ceased to be a child any more. I became aware of time and change and the sort of grief that is beyond the relief of tears.

The policeman who brought the news to us in Middlesex knocked heavily upon our door. My mother was speechless when she heard what he had come to say for she loved Grandmother. Her own mother had died when she was a girl and she knew the meaning of death which my father didn't know. Father buried his head in his hands when she told him his mother was dead. Mother began to hurry about the business of preparing his things for the journey home. Things that we had been doing until that moment became unimportant and drifted back like something falling on the surface of a swiftly flowing river. Grannie was dead. It wasn't yet spring and she had died without warning. There was no means of communicating with the family that were adequate to our needs. They had no telephone. A telegraph boy took half a day to go out from the town and come back with a message to be wired to us, and the thoughts we had were incoherent thoughts, ragged and shapeless like sheep on a hillside.

My father's things were packed, and mine too, for I had to be there. I was the eldest grandson, the eldest son of the only son, a principal mourner to be seen as a comfort to the older generation, some promise that although death took the old, the family lived on for ever. My mother hurried us off. We caught the first train north. I can't recall that my father spoke more than two words to me the whole way. He was lost in grief. In the early hours of the morning we rattled across the border and on towards Galloway. I already knew the route well. I had travelled it many times on my own. I loved the black outlines of firwoods, the humps of hills, the shadows of moorland even although I could see nothing distinctly. The air, the sounds of the echoes and the commotion of the train were all different because I was going back home. Grandmother was dead, but no one died when you could imagine them, when it was impossible to forget them, when you knew how they walked and talked and smiled, and the taste of the bread they baked and the jam they had given you on a saucer when they were testing it to see if it had jelled.

Death was a thing that people allowed themselves to believe in. I didn't believe in death yet but my father believed. By the time we had reached our destination he had the shocked countenance of the bereaved son. He was long past tears. We went out to the farm by a hired car for Grandfather was too full of grief to come for us. I breathed the cold air of the day and looked at the bright northern sky into which the returning geese were flying, and shivered because the car was unheated and had windows through which the wind blew. It had a smell of mildew and mud and horse manure, I remember, and had come out of the mews at the back of the Galloway Arms. It was long past being respectable enough for a funeral or a wedding and it was driven by a man in a cloth cap, who knew why we had come and who we were without asking or being told. He had looked my father in the eye when we met and solemnly clasped his hand.

We went up the steps to the door. My aunts turned their heads away from us and wept and went quickly back inside without exchanging a greeting of any kind. I sat in the kitchen and belonged nowhere for a while. Father went off to sit and talk to Grandfather who was in his armchair by the fire in the sitting-room, his head sunk on his chest. They were together for a long time. My aunts came and asked me if I was hungry and then set about preparing a meal. I began to understand that the world had changed. These were some of the really critical minutes of my life. I should have looked at the tree that lost its leaves and withered after it had been struck by lightning. I should have looked at the faces of people who had lost their relatives and understood that one spring isn't exactly the same as the last, and where grass grows it need not grow for ever.

At length my father came down and talked to his sisters. After we had eaten he took me by the hand and we went upstairs to see Grandmother, for the coffin-maker had been and the coffin was already in the house. It had been made by the joiner whose workshop was down the road. We went alone into the bedroom and when I had kissed my grandmother's cheek I knew the meaning of death. It was colder than anything in life and altogether unreal.

'Always look after your mother,' my father said, pressing my hand.

We went back downstairs and I went outside to look at the fields and let the clean, cold air freshen me. The peewits were calling on the ploughed land. It was mid March. The brightness of spring was unmistakable. I went off to see if I could find a peewit's nest. No one asked me where I was going or whether I was wearing clothes that might be ruined if I got caught on barbed wire or tumbled into a drain. The funeral, someone had said, would be the day after tomorrow. That would be soon enough considering Aunt Maggie had to come down from New Cumnock and cousins and second cousins at the other end of the shire had to make their arrangements for milking and other chores so that they could come. The peewits sailed round me and called and swept in to lure me where they could. I found one nest and then another, but I left the eggs where they were for who would cook them for breakfast at such a time? No one had any appetite at all. I hadn't as yet seen Grandfather. He hadn't sent for me, but when I returned to the house they told me that I must go and speak to him. I went down to the sitting-room and stood by his chair. He turned his head and looked at me and patted my head and I went back to the kitchen.

'What did your grandfather say to you?' asked my aunts. I shook my head and said he hadn't spoken. They stared out of the window and went on with what they were doing. Grandmother had died from some disorder of the heart, it seemed. It may have been a condition that was long-standing, but no one had ever thought that she suffered. She was seventy-six years old and this had been the only 'illness' she had suffered, except when she had broken a leg. The leg hadn't been splinted by the doctor. It had been fitted with a stool strapped on at the knee and adjusted so that she could get about while the bone or bones healed again. Miraculously this mishap had resulted in no complications. Her leg had mended perfectly. A broken leg was surely inadequate indication of frailty. She should have lived. People who worked hard and led a blameless life were expected to live, were entitled to live a long life. The shock of her death had thrown the household into confusion, into a sort of robot reaction that was more marked when friends and relatives arrived to express their sympathy. Grandmother had been respected and loved and Grandfather was well known. Even the family had no idea how many people were going to attend the funeral. There might, it seemed, be sixty or seventy but over a hundred farmers and other country people came to the funeral.

The undertaker had everything perfectly arranged. He handed little printed cards to each of the principal mourners. They bore the name of the person concerned on one side and a diagram of a coffin on the other with a number to indicate which position that mourner occupied when he took part in lowering the coffin into the grave. The number on the card I was given indicated that I was at the foot. My father was at the head, Grandfather and his brothers were on the other cords. I listened to the service and, when instructed, held on to the braided cord while the boards supporting the coffin above the grave were withdrawn. Slowly Grandmother was lowered into her last resting-place. The cord burned my hand. I tottered on the brink of the grave, filled with horror at the thought that if I let go the coffin would tumble and if I didn't, the uneven burden of weight would carry me into the grave. Someone reached out in time and steadied the cord in my hands and took the strain as Father and Grandfather and the others lowered the coffin. I went back to the farm with that gruesome card in my pocket and kept it for a long time, fascinated by the diagram and the number six against my name. There were no women at the funeral. It was not the custom in that part of the world to have women at funerals, only men, and a child became a man when circumstances made him a man. No one remarked that I had been assisted. I don't suppose my father or grandfather, in their grief, noticed that I was in danger of proving myself less than a man.

Grandfather went home to bed. He turned his face to the wall and said he would die. He no longer wanted to live, for all purpose had gone from his life. Grandmother had been everything to him, his prop, his comfort, his reassurance when he doubted himself. He knew that he would die without her. My father decided that I had better stay and be some sort of comfort, even a distraction, for the family. He took the train back south, glad to be gone and to forget his misery in work, but Grandfather was not to be distracted. He looked at the wall and refused to eat or take interest in anything. My aunts found the burden of responsibility heavy indeed. They talked to the rest of the family who came and tried to brighten the old man's spirits or encourage him to face up to life but he was inconsolable. He wanted to die and he almost had the determination to achieve it.

What excuses were made for my absence from school I don't know. I didn't care. I was free to walk the fields, to enjoy the spring and Easter days. Spring gave place to summer.

Grandfather stayed in bed and his daughters reproached him for being lazy, for being resigned to things as he had never been before in his life. It seemed to me that they were hard on him and upbraided him when they should have shown him sympathy and respect, but at last he could bear their nagging no longer and one day allowed himself to be chivvied downstairs and out of doors to look over the fields as he had always done. In a day or two he was plodding about and finding fault with everything that had been done while he had lain abed. Soon he was his old self again, winding the clocks, consulting his watch and predicting the weather for the next few hours or days. In a while he was back at market and going down to the smithy to mend something that the smiths couldn't manage, for this was something he had always greatly enjoyed. He attended the cattle shows and took the milk to the creamery, and had a stone put on Grandmother's grave. I was recalled to my father's house. I had hardly contributed at all to Grandfather's recovery, but I had certainly proved a distraction to my aunts for I had run wild with a vengeance and they had been hard put to it to prevent me from living a Huckleberry Finn existence in the woods and bogs, roasting blackbirds, or whatever birds I could snare or trap, and reverting to nature as I had always seemed about to do.

I suppose I must have recovered from the horror of my experience on the day that Grandmother was buried before I returned home, but I never forgot that journey to the cemetery with the seemingly endless procession of cars, gigs and people on foot who had all come to pay their respects to the dead and the living. No one to whom I tried to convey my experience on that occasion seemed to understand how frightened I had been. The custom of lowering a relative into the grave isn't now widely observed, I think, and it is one that could inflict greater anguish on the mourners than any other ritual invented by undertakers. It wasn't observed at Grandfather's funeral, when his time came, and I don't think I have ever heard of it since. Perhaps it was a custom falling into disuse and abandoned in that part of the world long after it had been given up elsewhere. I wish I had preserved the card, but the memory of that occasion was seared upon my mind as with a hot iron on my flesh. All the others who lowered the coffin that day are dead now.

Grandfather survived Grandmother by ten years. He died quite peacefully in his bed one afternoon, died after smoking his pipe as his father had done. Great-grandfather had remarked after he put his pipe away that he would take a little sleep and he took a long endless sleep, dying as men who live in peace deserve to die, without torment. I was no longer a child. If I cried at all I cried inwardly and cried for the world as it had been. The old man's dog cried, I was told, a long, pitiful cry that marked the moment of his death after which the grief stricken animal rushed out of doors and stayed in the fields and woods for days. Again the countryside came in droves to pay their respects. The ritual, as I have said, changed a little. I cannot recall that my father and grandfather stood to shake hands with the mourners before the funeral began. Perhaps they did, but my father and I stood side by side at the door of the farmhouse while the undertaker's men marshalled the company and they came in single file past us to shake hands, old men, farmers, labourers, gamekeepers, the mole-catcher, the shepherds and ploughmen, the village grocer, the miller, the joiner, all the world. It was a sad and unreal occasion.

The women of the household were busy within, preparing a funeral tea that everyone would try to eat if they could manage to get back to their farms in time for milking. Uncle Peter and Uncle Charlie were at hand to help with any problems that the womenfolk might have but my father had urgent business that required his departure as soon as he could return south. Nothing is for ever and everything changes. There were fewer gigs and more cars in the cortege. The problem that loomed on the immediate horizon was how adequately two women and a beardless boy could run the farm, even with the advice of relatives and friends. There is a time to die and Grandfather had lived his time.

He was to have retired, it was said. He had talked about retiring, but those who knew how he loved the place knew that he couldn't tear himself away. He belonged there in spirit and nothing could uproot him. Nostalgia never troubled him for he was never long parted from the place. It troubled me and it is surely a disease that is hard to shake off when it begins when childhood ends. I might have been a farmer. I had ploughed the land. I had harrowed the newly sown fields, rolled them and cut the crop with reaper or binder. I had built ricks, helped doctor cattle and shared every sort of work that was done, but I had picked up a pen to write and somehow cut myself off from my peasant heritage. I thought long and hard about it while I divorced myself from what might have been my proper vocation.

The author, John McNeillie with his Grandfather and Grandmother at North Clutag.

I wonder if I really belonged in the practical world of the farmer at all? A man must see the corn in his imagination when he plants it and feel the quality of the grain in his hand while he still runs the harrows over the field. He must have his visions, develop his imagination and go forward hopefully to cultivate his dreams. Nostalgia of the kind that has prompted this book, for instance, depends on things remaining fixed in the mind, coloured in the imagination, changing only to seem bigger and brighter and better than they really were. I need not say that as a child in Galloway I was happy and that although I have been happy since I have never been happier than I was then. The Galloway of my childhood is no more. The people who belonged in it have gone. No one who writes about life does life justice by being a realist. The fields were greener, the trees were taller, the spots on the trout I caught were the most brilliant red you could ever imagine, and the curlew's cry would have broken your heart and you will never hear its like, now or ever. You must take my word for that.